The Imperfectionists

STRATEGIC MINDSETS for UNCERTAIN TIMES

The Imperfectionists

STRATEGIC MINDSETS for UNCERTAIN TIMES

Robert McLean   Charles Conn

Bestselling Authors of *Bulletproof Problem Solving*

WILEY

Published by John Wiley & Sons, Inc., Hoboken, New Jersey.
Published simultaneously in Canada.

For general information on our other products and services or for technical support, please contact our Customer Care Department within the United States at (800) 762-2974, outside the United States at (317) 572-3993 or fax (317) 572-4002.

Wiley also publishes its books in a variety of electronic formats. Some content that appears in print may not be available in electronic formats. For more information about Wiley products, visit our web site at www.wiley.com.

Library of Congress Cataloging-in-Publication Data is Available:

ISBN 9781119835660 (Hardback)
ISBN 9781119835684 (ePDF)
ISBN 9781119835677 (ePub)

Cover image(s): © Pablo Prat/Shutterstock; © Olivier Le Moal/Shutterstock
Cover design: Wiley

SKY10043652_022823

Contents

Introduction: Becoming an Imperfectionist

If you are an Amazon customer, chances are you have encountered household names such as Amazon Fresh, Amazon Prime, Audible, and Zappos. It's less likely that you would have noted the baby steps Amazon took to expand beyond its core business into consumer financial services. The acquisition of TextPayMe, the investment in Bill Me Later, the hiring of a team from GoPayGo, and the launch of a remote card payment device, Amazon Local Register, were modest moves that involved only small financial outlay and attracted relatively little attention at the time. They also all ended in apparent failure, with TextPayMe (rebranded Amazon Web Pay) closing in 2014, Local Register withdrawing from the market in the face of competition from Square, and Bill Me Later being acquired by rival PayPal.

Yet today Amazon is a powerhouse in consumer finance, boasting a 24% user share in the United States for its pan-economy Amazon Pay service, and is positioned to develop further as a global finance player. How did the company craft success at scale from a series of pint-sized and seemingly unpromising moves? The answer is that Amazon is an *imperfectionist*, a concept we've developed over several decades of helping companies and nonprofits, and one that we believe is vital for all organizations, big and small, striving to prosper in today's uniquely uncertain economic environment.

On the face of it being an imperfectionist doesn't sound like a good thing. We certainly don't mean accepting things that are faulty, a common meaning of imperfection. What we *do* mean is tolerating ambiguity and acknowledging that certainty and perfection, however desirable they may seem, come at too high a cost for problem solvers in uncertain times. Imperfectionists step into risk, proceeding through trial and error, utilizing small moves and other tools to deepen their understanding of the nature of the game being played, and then thoughtfully move forward into uncertainty. Imperfectionism has intellectual roots in the phrase attributed to the eighteenth-century French philosopher Voltaire: "Don't let perfect be the enemy of good." It is also resonant with the Japanese aesthetic known as *wabi sabi*, which is the acceptance of imperfection and impermanence.

Amazon approached the challenge of entering unfamiliar consumer finance markets through small company purchases, team hires, and partnerships. Along the way it built valuable capabilities and assets, learned from its mistakes, and reduced the risks of later, bigger moves. It stepped into risk and laid the foundation of a large new business brick by brick, rather than using its giant balance sheet to buy a consumer finance brand or a bank. This step-by-step approach was no accident—Amazon followed the same modus operandi in commercial finance and in its creation and dominance of cloud computing, and is now doing something similar in healthcare.

> "From very early on in Amazon's life, we knew we wanted to create a culture of builders—people who are curious, explorers. . . . Even when they're experts, they are 'fresh' with a beginner's mind. . . . A builder's mentality helps us approach big, hard-to-solve opportunities with a humble conviction that success can come through iteration: invent, launch, reinvent, relaunch, start over, rinse, repeat, again and again. They know the path to success is anything but straight."—Amazon 2015 Annual Report

Many organizations are responding to today's extremely uncertain post-COVID environment by taking hasty bets, including "leap-before-you-look" acquisitions (think Robert Redford and Paul Newman jumping off the cliff in the movie *Butch Cassidy and the Sundance Kid*). Elon Musk's acquisition of Twitter may fit this mold. Bank of America's disastrous $40 billion acquisition of subprime lender Countrywide Financial in 2008, which quickly turned into a legal and financial nightmare and landed the leading US bank with an estimated $51 billion in losses, is a good example of the risks of rash behavior.

Other companies are succumbing to risk-aversion paralysis, a mistake even more common than swashbuckling misadventure. We continue to see many management teams stuck in a "wait and see" mindset, not moving quickly enough to confront and ride the ever-shifting tide of global economic forces. Remember video retailer Blockbuster, proud owner of more than 9,000 stores and employer of more than 84,000 people in 2004? It failed to respond to digital subscription services like Netflix and eventually filed for bankruptcy in 2010. You can't hide from disruptive risk.

Imperfectionism is an idea that stands opposed to both of these costly extremes. Between the extremes of "bet the farm" Bank of America and "do nothing" Blockbuster is a sweet spot where imperfectionists play, employing a set of strategic mindsets and problem solving tools that master uncertainty. This book's purpose is to help business leaders and their nonprofit equivalents to discover these mindsets, be more confident and creative about problem solving in uncertain times, and be successful where others are afraid to act, or act recklessly.

This book on problem solving under uncertainty is really a book about strategy. While we believe it is sensible to develop high-level strategies based on an organization's objectives and an understanding of structural market and competitive forces, we believe that most business strategy is fantasy. Market conditions and disruptive entry are changing too quickly for armchair planning based on certainty to be useful. Organizations need to be nimble imperfectionists, tolerating ambiguity and weighing the odds, constantly experimenting, and stepping out into risk, not moving pieces on some theoretical gameboard. Imperfectionism is strategy in action.

The Context: Massive Change and Uncertainty

For all of human history up to the years just before the twentieth century, not much changed for most people. Ever. Nearly everyone was born into the same roles as their mothers and fathers, overwhelmingly in agriculture. Thanks to fear of famine, innovation and productivity grew incredibly slowly. Our ancestors faced risk and uncertainty, to be sure, but of perennial and anticipated kinds: hunger, disease, war.

Then in the past 100 or so years everything changed. Now, we barely recognize our grandparents' lives, let alone the lives of those who went before them. Uncertainty still includes deprivation, sickness, and conflict for many on the planet, but now uncertainty comes in dozens of other forms, from social media to nuclear fusion, from artificial intelligence to quantum computing. Many of these innovations are largely forces for good: Who could have imagined that disabled people could manipulate objects with their minds, or that novel mRNA vaccines could be developed in less than a year? Some innovations will reduce drudgery and make working conditions safer—but without question most have led to a massive disruption of traditional jobs and of institutions that we once took for granted.

The rate of production of new knowledge and communications is overwhelming (see Exhibit I.1).[1] More new information has been created since 2010 than in all of previous human history. Stop and think about that. It is impossible for even the most talented people to stay abreast of this wave. Even the polymath Newtons, Bacons, and Rousseaus of our age cannot begin to keep up with the race of new knowledge and its impact on our organizations and lives.

Artificial intelligence, automation, programmable biology, robotics, and other technologies are transforming every industry. The rate of disruption is overturning market leaders more quickly than ever and installing new top competitors, often from entirely outside that industry. There is not a single company in the Dow Jones Index today that was there at the inception of the Index in 1885. The average life span of companies in the S&P 500 was 61 years in 1958; today it is 18.

Regulators cannot hope to guide and manage the enormously powerful companies that now extend across industries and geographies, many of them spawned by winner-takes-all network economics. The speed of

ACCELERATING CHANGE & UNCERTAINTY

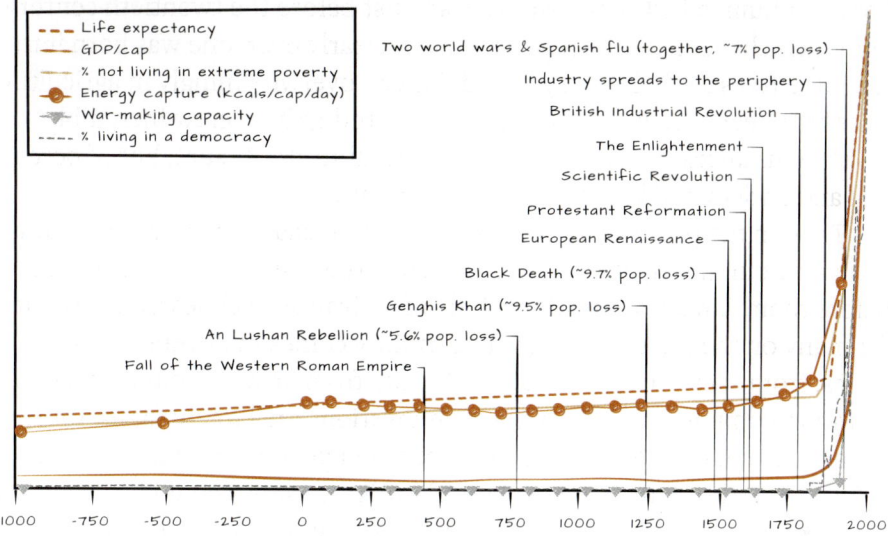

Exhibit I.1

SOURCE: LUKE MUEHLHAUSER.

expansion and the scale of investment is breathtaking: Just look at the pace to $1 billion in sales for recent internet media winners. Faster and faster (see Exhibit I.2).[2]

These disruptive technologies have a stark human as well as financial cost, destroying many of today's jobs, and not just at the manual end. Software and AI challenge everyone in the middle, as well as previously protected professions like the law, banking, medicine, dentistry, and programming. Software is eating the world, Marc Andreessen famously said—and now AI is eating software programming jobs. These technologies also create new jobs, of course, but the new roles are often inherently more fluid and less certain. As we will explain in this book, imperfectionism and its sister mindsets can provide the capability edge for individuals competing for such jobs.

Most new careers didn't exist 10 years ago, and many won't exist 10 years from now. No one will do the same thing for a lifetime as our grandparents did. In this vastly more complicated world, how can we and the organizations we work for be competitive? How can we shape strategies

INCREASING PACE OF CHANGE: REVENUE PATH OF
INTERNET START-UPS

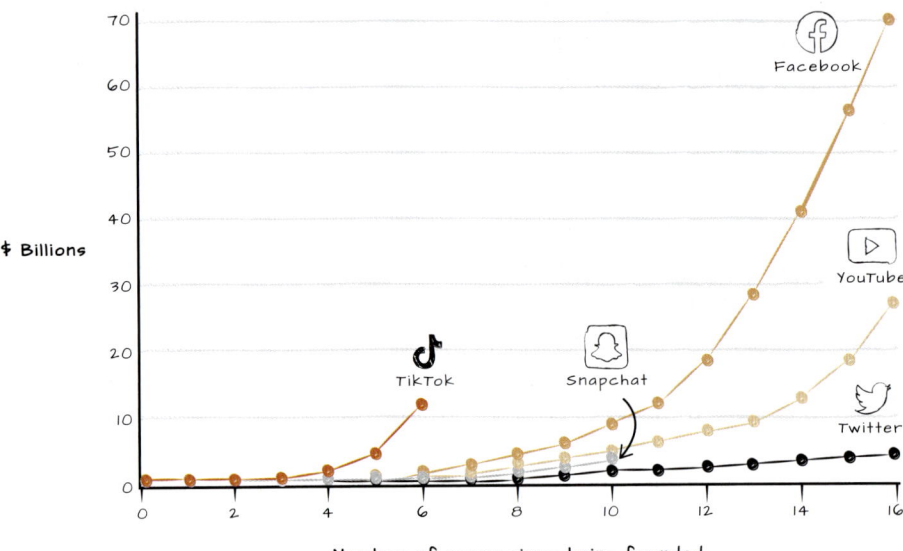

Exhibit I.2
SOURCE: CHARTR.

that allow us to be successful? How can we be creative disruptors rather
than those who end up on the dust-heap of the disrupted?

Problem Solving Toolsets and Mindsets

One of the things that humans do better than artificial intelligence does is
to creatively solve problems in teams—and the good news is that this
should continue to be the case for some time. Today most machine
learning and AI is good at sophisticated pattern recognition, not creative
or truly generative problem solving. Pattern recognition may help develop
unexpected strategies in chess or Go, but these are games with little or no
uncertainty except the opponent's next move. Humans have the edge in
creativity for now. No one can predict the future, but you can be ready for
it if you combine a disciplined toolset for problem solving with powerful
and mutually reinforcing strategic mindsets.

In our first book, *Bulletproof Problem Solving: The One Skill That Changes Everything*, we presented a seven-step toolset for structured problem solving (for an introduction to this model, see the Appendix). In this new book we will show how Imperfectionism and its sister mindsets can give you and your organization an even bigger advantage in this topsy-turvy new world. Logically, the mindsets around problem solving precede the toolset you employ, and are ultimately more important. The way you think about the future, how you gather and process information to make judgments to inform action, is fundamental to your success. Simply put, an imperfectionist mindset creates opportunities not available to those with conventional thinking.

The term *mindset* has been in use since the 1930s, but has received lasting attention in the work of psychologist Carol Dweck. Her distinction between growth mindsets and fixed mindsets is insightful, but our research into problem solving over three decades has allowed us to go beyond this simple dialectic and look at the mindsets that characterize nimble problem solvers.

Most dictionary definitions of mindset focus on a mental attitude or inclination, especially those that are habitual. Our working definition is different:

> A mindset is an orientation toward new information about future states that provides a favorable vantage point for action.

In this definition a mindset is a way of thinking that allows the risks generated by uncertainty to be managed and successful actions to be undertaken. Mindsets are not the same as positive or wishful thinking; their power lies in the way they encourage this orientation toward the future, and in their contribution to driving better outcomes. They stand in stark contrast to the static bodies of information still taught by many educational institutions on the assumption that we will have a single career of four decades or more, just as our grandparents did, rather than multiple roles across several industries. The best training for the jobs of tomorrow is creative problem solving tools and mindsets.

We have been working together on problem solving in complex environments for 30 years, first on business and nonprofit problems at McKinsey & Company, later as entrepreneurs and advisors to start-ups, and finally on the large-scale problems of environment and society as board members of foundations and NGOs, including as fellow Regional Council members at The Nature Conservancy. In the past decade we have conducted focused research with teams at Oxford University and the University of Sydney on the mechanics and mindsets of great problem solving.

The six mindsets we explore and explain here are like old companions who have been on a long journey together but haven't had their names called out until now. It took the paralyzing uncertainty most organizations faced in responding to COVID-19 for us to fully appreciate their value in an age of extreme and increasing uncertainty. Along the way we encountered some remarkable and at times surprising examples of problem solving, from how unschooled woodworker John Harrison cracked the longitude problem to how parson Thomas Bayes uncovered the power of conditional probability in responding to uncertain events.

We wrote this book as a practical guide to help you understand, assess, and embrace risk, and to solve hard problems with creativity and boldness. In short, to allow you to harness the power of imperfectionism—to be an imperfectionist.

Six Mindsets for Problem Solving under Uncertainty

We have already introduced Imperfectionism, one of the mindsets we believe is critical for understanding and then stepping into uncertainty. Imperfectionism is also our overarching term for this set of six mindsets for embracing risk. Some of the other mindsets we describe, like curiosity, will be familiar; others, like occurrent behavior, less so. However, the six mindsets in total and in combination should allow those who adopt them to navigate the seas of unknown unknowns and to leave behind the comfort of corporate certainty, expert knowledge, historical data, and pyramid-structured presentations—most of the things we learned in university and in our early careers.

That's right, we are saying that in times of rapid change, you should be curious, embrace risk and not avoid it, you should be suspicious of experts, you should think about how to run your own experiments, you should consider ways to source ideas from entirely different fields, and you should convince your colleagues that you have the right answer with rich and visual storytelling that speaks to their values rather than to logic alone.

Most companies and nonprofits still assume away uncertainty—think of all those budget forecasts and strategy documents with no mention of potential disruption from unexpected events, or deliberately constructed with a lackluster upside and downside case to focus attention on the base case. The related pathology is paralysis by uncertainty, a dogged attachment to business as usual, waiting for the certainty that never comes. In both cases organizations are unprepared for disruptive new entrants and fresh sources of competition. Warren Buffett tells us to be fearful when others are greedy, and greedy when others are fearful, but most of us go along with the herd . . . and then get picked off by the lions.

Combing through our research spanning hundreds of problem types, we have distilled six mindsets that will help you avoid this fate. Let's take a look at them (see Exhibit I.3).

Ever Curious

Young children still learning the patterns of the world are relentless askers of the question "Why?" Unfortunately, as we get older, and solve basic problems like how to tie a shoelace, we rein in our curiosity. Pattern seekers in youth, we become pattern imposers in later life as we become more certain that we know the answer to everything. Recognizing patterns is useful in many circumstances (driver: curve coming up, slow down), but it is deadly for problem solving in situations of high uncertainty. Why? Because we often get the pattern wrong when things are changing quickly.

We assume, for example, that a strategy that has always worked will continue to work. Charles ran a start-up online city guide company called Citysearch in the 1990s. The company was up against century-old dominant newspapers. They had survived the entry of radio and television, and they knew they would survive this upstart internet thing. They knew the bases of media competition: Hire brilliant writers and create wonderful content, build readership, and dominate local advertising. But in actual fact, the bases of competition in local media were changing, and changing fast.

The internet allowed users to *generate their own content* and share it with each other, and with a variety and creativity that could never be matched in broadsheet print. Worse, thanks to superior searching and

MINDSETS FOR PROBLEM SOLVING UNDER UNCERTAINTY

Being an **imperfectionist** with a high tolerance for **ambiguity**

Practicing **show and tell**, recognizing that storytelling begets action

Being **ever curious** about every element of your problem

6 MUTUALLY REINFORCING MINDSETS

Tapping into **collective intelligence**, acknowledging that the smartest people are not in the room

Having a **dragonfly eye** view of the world, to see through multiple lenses

Pursuing **occurrent behavior** with restless experimenting

Exhibit I.3

matching, valuable classified advertising for cars, jobs, homes, and personal ads actually works better online. Newspapers produced remarkable content, and had rich advertising franchises. They likely could have been effective competitors in the new world had they been more curious about the internet and about how local media strategies would have to change.

On the whole, they weren't. With falling readership and declining advertising revenues, editorial staffs were slashed, leading to a further downward spiral in readership and economics. Today only a small set of newspapers are vibrant businesses.

Curiosity is an essential orientation for problem solving in uncertain times. Managers must be able to suspend their natural pattern recognition impulses long enough to see evolving challenges in a fresh light, especially when uncertainty is not just about known patterns (it will rain, it will not rain), but instead is governed by entirely novel events. When great problem solvers seek to close the gap between what they know and what they need to know, curiosity reduces uncertainty. That may strike some readers as counterintuitive. Particularly in uncertain times, wouldn't it be better to bridle curiosity, and try to moor in certainty? In our experience such a recipe is likely to be steamrolled by change.

Dragonfly Eye

Our pattern-imposing brains evolved in a dangerous world where quick decisions were required to stay alive. Rustling leaves triggered rapid pattern recognition (predator, run). But dangers four million years ago only came in a few varieties. With massive changes in technology, there is now a kaleidoscope of possibilities. In this new environment there is huge value in testing several different perspectives on each problem, rather than assuming it is business as usual.

We call this mindset the dragonfly eye, a term we first learned from Philip Tetlock and Dan Gardner's work on superforecasters. Dragonflies have huge compound eyes, with hundreds of lenses that are sensitive to different wavelengths of light. We do not know exactly how their insect brains process all this visual information, but we do know that they gather much more data than our human eyes, perceiving colors and movement unseen by us. By analogy, when faced with new and uncertain information, great problem solvers try on several different lenses in an effort to understand the problem. They zoom in and then zoom out, or widen the aperture to make sure they are seeing the real structure in front of them, and are not imposing an old solution or addressing its surface.

Take Peloton, a home exercise company started by one of Charles's former Citysearch colleagues, John Foley. The company has recently experienced major post-pandemic growing pains, to be sure. But it was by viewing the home exercise market through an entirely different lens than other people that Foley gained the insight that led to him starting this fresh and exciting business. Historically, the aim of most home gym equipment companies has been to bring outside exercise inside, say by propping up a bike to make it stationary, or creating a treadmill to simulate outdoor running. Foley saw it differently. He realized people wanted to recreate not just the movements of exercise outside the home, but the whole social environment of exercise classes, led by inspirational trainers. No one had seen home exercise through this lens before, leading to the introduction of remote participation in exercise classes via streaming media, and a $50 billion company valuation at one point during the pandemic.

We have been curious about the rise in obesity, a substantial human health crisis in many countries that has all the characteristics of a "wicked problem" (complex reinforcing causality). For some, obesity is simple: too many calories in, too few out, leading to public health interventions like the banning of large-sized sugary soft drinks, as Michael Bloomberg tried to do while he was mayor of New York City. We know those kinds of interventions don't work, so a few years ago we worked with a group of students in Oxford to develop alternative perspectives using multiple regression analysis across cities. The exercise confirmed what social scientists have suspected for some time: Income and other social determinants have a huge impact on obesity. Later, a Bayesian analysis by a multi-faceted team sponsored by the Paul Ramsay Foundation in Australia showed that the strongest determinants of obesity were related to social disadvantage, and in particular to the level of schooling of the mother. As a result of what was learned looking through this lens, public policy now has the challenge of keeping lower-income girls in school longer.

The point of this mindset is to see beyond the familiar tropes into which our pattern-recognizing brains want to assemble perceptions. By changing the lens or widening the aperture, we can identify threats or opportunities beyond the periphery of our conventional vision.

Occurrent Behavior

Occurrent behavior is an odd term, but we like it. It means watching what actually happens in a time and place, not what was desired or predicted.

Great problem solvers go beyond conventional historical data to explore whether they can observe new evidence about a problem, sometimes by running experiments to test hypotheses, or, where that isn't possible, by looking for natural experiments. If we don't gather new data, as Canadian media theorist Marshall McLuhan said, we are driving into the future using only our rearview mirror.

The internet has made this kind of direct, current experimentation easier for many organizations. A/B testing is now a standard way to assess any new product launch or promotion. By partitioning your online audience into two or more segments with otherwise similar characteristics, and then testing different versions of the new product or promotion on each, you can draw lessons from the responses. Airtasker, an Australian online company that allows online users to outsource everyday tasks, tested five versions of a booking fee before implementing one that immediately generated a huge revenue gain. Six months later it ran a trial featuring an even higher booking fee, immediately learning that a clear price/volume threshold existed (their revenue went down!) and confirming the original choice.

Although it is harder and more expensive to do this sort of testing in physical product markets, it's possible and often worthwhile. Patagonia, for example, works with professional athletes to gather data on new products, tweaking and perfecting them before launch. The approach led to significant changes ahead of the launch of new mountain-biking shorts. Sometimes the company releases a product in a small market to gather additional data before offering it across their whole network. Clever companies analyze lots of new data before making expensive, irreversible decisions.

Sometimes it isn't possible to construct new tests because it would be unethical for one of the control groups. Then good problem solvers look for *natural experiments*, where similar groups get different solutions for other reasons, such as from different administrations in twin cities or similar countries. Alternative medications, treatment policies, and pandemic control measures have created a large number of natural experiments in the past two pandemic years. Neighboring Sweden and Norway, for instance, which have similar population demographics, followed different pandemic control policies, which led to substantially different mortality outcomes.

The occurrent behavior mindset, underpinned intellectually by the insights of Thomas Bayes, an eighteenth-century statistician and clergyman, is best thought of as a willingness to experiment relentlessly via conscious trial and error and to use that new information to update prior understanding. This mindset is in short supply in many organizations, often because managers are fearful of looking stupid for changing strategies.

Collective Intelligence

Bill Joy, one of the founders of Sun Microsystems, once observed that the smartest people are usually working for someone else. His solution was to find ways to have these clever people "labor in his garden." Open-source software development is a brilliant way to get the smartest folks to work on a common problem, and this was the heart of the development of Unix, the core programming architecture that is now found in almost every commercial software solution.

Those with a collective intelligence mindset accept that it's unlikely that the best people to solve a problem for their organization can be found solely inside its four walls. The conventional response is often to hire an expert, and on the surface that makes sense. The expert consulting model is one we are very familiar with. And it made a lot of sense in the 1960s, 1970s, and 1980s for sectors with relatively stable players and core technologies such as big steel, big mining, and other traditional industries. In these cases it was relatively straightforward to improve performance by learning from experts who had helped achieve cost reductions or make capital investment more efficient at another site.

All that goes out the window when technological change accelerates and industries are rocked by disruptive entrants, as is true in almost every field today, including heavy industry. Even as long ago as 1968, Nucor Steel put the rest of the US steel industry on the back foot with the introduction of its new electric arc furnace, fed by iron and steel scrap. Industry incumbents who relied too heavily on experts schooled in the integrated iron and steel industry ended up fighting (and losing) the last war.

Clever organizations now cast their nets more broadly, involving people with diverse skills who may have never thought about their business. For example, The Nature Conservancy (TNC) turned to crowd-sourcing firm Kaggle in its search for a machine learning algorithm to identify fish catch species and quantities on fishing boats. By offering a prize of $150,000 for the best solution, it attracted entries from 2,293 teams from all over the world. TNC now uses the winning algorithm to protect endangered Pacific tuna and other species.

Sometimes collective intelligence requires going back to the future. With climate change leading to unprecedented fire management challenges in many countries, resource agency officials are now tapping into the traditional knowledge of indigenous populations, who coexisted with and harnessed fire for thousands of generations before modern technical fire management. This collective ancestral wisdom, long ignored, is now changing practices across a number of countries with similar savannah grasslands.

The collective intelligence mindset is a close sister to the multiple lens-seeking dragonfly eye mindset. It compels us to look for creative solutions to fast-moving problems from a diverse range of sources outside our organization.

Imperfectionism

When we think of great problem solvers, many of us picture a brilliant engineer, a confident mastermind who knows what they are doing and approaches the challenge with determined precision. The reality is that good problem solving under uncertainty requires assessing the odds through trial and error—it's more like the unruly flow of a rugby game than linear programming.

As with Amazon's stepwise entry into consumer financial services, savvy problem solvers do their best to understand the structure and competitive dynamics of an industry, develop initial entry strategies, and then make small moves that further illuminate the characteristics of the game. They build capabilities, sometimes through experience, sometimes by hiring competitors' teams. They add intellectual property and other business assets as they go, and gradually ready themselves for larger moves. They manage risk by hedging and laying it off on others when they can. These problem solvers accept that some of their moves will fail. That's okay as long as the costs are reasonable, the consequences are reversible, and lessons are learned from the less successful experiments.

We developed our understanding of this imperfection mindset a number of years ago, noticing, for example, the deft entry of Johnson & Johnson into the lucrative contact lens market via a series of small knowledge- and skill-building moves. The end result is what we call a growth staircase or horizon, a framework for prethinking strategic moves in businesses or nonprofits.

> *"There are scientific ways to address a new idea or project. If you take the conservative scientific route, you study the problem in your head or on paper until you are sure there is no chance of failure. However, you have taken so long that the competition has already beaten you to market. The entrepreneurial way is to immediately take a forward step and if that feels good, take another; if not, step back. Learn by doing, it is a faster process."*
> —Yvon Chouinard, founder of Patagonia

Imperfectionists seek to map out a path through murky conditions, resisting the urge to make the sort of "bet the farm" acquisitions that destroy value, and equally refusing to be paralyzed by uncertainty. Our friends and former colleagues Tim Koller and Dan Lovallo have shown in a series of real-world simulations that middle managers in established firms won't take winning risk-adjusted bets. It is these companies whose markets are ripe for disruption in a world awash with capital. Economist Joseph Schumpeter wrote his insightful opus about capitalism's potential for creative destruction in the 1940s, but things are moving even faster nowadays.

You'll recognize imperfectionists by the way they talk comfortably about the odds and how these can be improved through careful learning steps or laying off risk on others. They are emboldened by trial and error. They happily embrace "epistemic humility" about what is knowable at any point in time. As we will see throughout the chapters of this book, they use the other five mindsets to gather novel perspectives and data to guide their thoughtful moves.

Show and Tell

We started our discussion of mindsets with a reference to children and curiosity, and we return to children now with the "show and tell" mindset. As you no doubt remember—from back in the days when you were more curious—show and tell is an elementary-school activity. It's not usually associated with problem solving, but in our experience it's often a critical support to creative thinking. Show and tell enables you to connect an audience with the problem and then use combinations of logic and persuasion to get results.

Facts and data have enormous appeal. Presented in the tight logic of the pyramid argument structure developed by journalists (and codified by Barbara Minto in *The Pyramid Principle*), they compel audiences to see the wisdom of strategies for our toughest problems. But as new information has mushroomed in the internet age, people are overwhelmed. Partisans weaponize data, with the result that no one knows what bits of information or arguments to trust. Cynicism, even inside otherwise apolitical organizations, often sets in.

Rookie problem solvers show you their analytic processes and mathematics to convince you that they are clever, sometimes known as APK (the anxious parade of knowledge). Seasoned problem solvers, as Nobel Prize winner Herb Simon observed, do it differently and more elegantly, representing the problem "so as to make the solution transparent." There is a reason for the aphorism that a picture is worth a thousand words: Humans are visual learners.

Great problem solvers are storytellers who are clear about the action that should flow from the findings, the governing idea for change. They then find a way to present their logic visually, so that the path to answers can be viscerally understood, debated, and embraced. They set out their case emotionally as well as logically, connecting with the values of their audience, and show why their preferred action offers an attractive balance between risks and rewards. As Jonathan Haidt's work on values and polarization has demonstrated, *frames beat facts*.

Is Your Organization an Imperfectionist?

Looking at their antitheses, or opposites, is a good way to understand better what we mean by each of the six mindsets described in this book. If your organization answers to one or more of the descriptors in the right-hand column of Exhibit I.4, alarm bells should start to ring.

ANCHORING THE MINDSETS

6 Problem solving mindsets	Antithesis of these mindsets
1. Imperfectionist	Certainty and perfection
2. Ever Curious	Closed mind
3. Dragonfly Eye	Single lens perspective
4. Occurrent behaviour	Reliance on past data and models
5. Collective intelligence	Believe the smartest people are in the room
6. Show & tell	Logic and facts rule

Exhibit I.4

Mindsets Together

Each of the mindsets for problem solving under uncertainty fights a common enemy: Our pattern-seeking minds have the potential to lead us astray when the situation our pattern-recognizing brains trained on no longer prevails. When the world is changing quickly, a great problem solving approach is to slow down and notice the nature of the new environment. This starts with curiosity—wondering why, asking questions. It then moves to seeing things through multiple lenses or angles, trying on alternative potential framings. Next, it seeks novel data on the emerging world via fresh experimentation, rather than relying on experts or older structured information. It augments this new data when required by crowdsourcing potential solutions from outside the obvious fields or sources. This curiosity, structured perspective taking, and new data generation in turn leads to a pragmatic plan to edge into uncertainty, gathering more information through small moves, adding capabilities and assets, and learning from mistakes and successes—that is imperfectionism, not waiting for certainty. Finally, clever strategic problem solving rallies others to support your plans with visual storytelling, not just facts and logic.

These strategic mindsets for solving tough problems in the risky circumstances of high uncertainty help you fight the decision biases inherent in being human, and give you the data to develop informed strategies to win. In the fast-changing world we all find ourselves in, being an imperfectionist is a critical advantage for you and your organization.

Chapter 1
Ever Curious

"Can I see the photograph, Daddy?"

Edwin Land was a brilliant scientist whose early inventions included Polaroid sunglasses and photographic filters. He later developed valuable cutting-edge technology that was used in World War II. Yet it took a simple question from his three-year-old daughter to unlock the key to perhaps his most famous discovery of all, the instant camera.

In 1943 Land and the young Jennifer were holidaying in Santa Fe, New Mexico, walking the streets and taking photographs along the way. It was decades before the advent of smartphones, digital cameras, or even the first "Fotomat" drop-off kiosk, and tourist "snaps" at the time took several days or even weeks to come back from the lab. For most consumers, the inconvenience of not knowing straightaway whether they had blinked or scowled was a small price to pay for the miracle of being able to distill a moment into a paper-thin memento. But Land's inquisitive daughter felt otherwise.

"Can I see the photograph, Daddy?" Jennifer asked after her father's index finger triggered the shutter of his 1941 Kodak. Unbeknownst to her, the young child had precipitated one of the great inventions of the twentieth century. Land was immediately taken by the concept of instant photography and set off on a long walk to think through the idea. He would later reflect:

> "As I walked around that charming town I undertook the task of solving the puzzle she had set me. Within the hour, the camera, the film, and the physical chemistry became so clear to me that with a great sense of excitement I hurried over to the place where Donald Brown, our Patent Attorney (in Santa Fe by coincidence) was staying, to describe to him in great detail a dry camera which would give a picture immediately after exposure."[1]

Land got to work creating Polaroid's first instant camera, the Model 95, which was launched in 1948. Polaroid instant cameras became an enormous commercial success.

Curiosity is our first and, in many ways, most foundational mindset for solving problems under great uncertainty. Without curiosity, inventors like Land would become pedestrian and fall well short of their creative potential. Asking "Why is it so?" is the key instinct for those who push beyond conventional answers, especially when the world feels unstable and uncertain.

Understanding Curiosity

Nobel prize winner Barry Marshall recounts a personal tale of curiosity: When he was 13 years old, he and his brother Bill read about an experiment with balloons in the *Newnes Popular Encyclopedia*. Curious to find out more, they could not resist the temptation to try to replicate it:

> *"We took an empty 4 gallon kerosene drum and soldered some connections to it so that we could fill it with house gas (propane) and then connect a balloon on the top and the water hose on the bottom, to drive the gas into the balloon, making a lighter-than-air balloon (we couldn't get helium in those days). However, we had not totally expelled all the air out of the drum, so we ended up with a highly flammable mixture of gas and air. My father pointed this out to us and demonstrated by touching a cigarette to a balloon. It was many weeks before his eyebrows grew back after being enveloped in a ball of flame!"*[2]

While we all know curiosity when we see it, it can be hard to define. Psychologists have been working for decades to provide an answer. Curiosity, they say, is the desire to close a gap between what you know and what you want to know. Psychologist George Loewenstein, argues that curiosity functions like a "drive state."[3] We are all familiar with drive states, even if we are not aware of the term. An obvious example is the desire to eat.

When great problem solvers seek to close the gap between what they know and what they want to know, curiosity *reduces* the uncertainty. That may strike some readers as counterintuitive. Particularly in uncertain times, wouldn't it be better to rein in curiosity, and try to anchor in certainty? What does curiosity have to do with uncertainty? A lot, it turns out.

Children, Curiosity, and Uncertainty

Research shows us that curiosity is a universal innate trait of infants and small children. Babies are enormously curious, and become more so through the first months and years of their lives. They explore their world, learning its patterns and developing and testing theories of what works.[4] First with sound and smell, then eyes and fingers, then mouth, often in partnership with parents and caregivers. The 2- to 5-year-old is always asking why, always testing what is known and reaching for what they want to know. We love the expression "childlike" curiosity. Some 4-year-olds are known to ask 200–300 questions per day. Little wonder that their loving parents are exhausted. From ages 5 to 12, curiosity diminishes rapidly as fewer everyday events bring surprises and the number of developed schemas (worked-out answers) increases.

Child psychology researchers have pinpointed a mid-level of uncertainty—a "sweet spot" that is neither particularly low nor remarkably high—that is distinctly associated with curiosity in babies. Too little uncertainty, or too much, and a baby turns away, bored on the one hand, overstimulated or afraid on the other.[5] This finding chimes with our own observations of problem solvers. When something is reasonably certain, or when a future event, such as a large meteorite hitting the earth, is highly uncertain, there is less need for curiosity. But once there is a middling degree of uncertainty, problem solving juices start to flow. That's when effective problem solvers can attack a problem with a reasonable expectation of success (see Exhibit 1.1).[6]

Curiosity in children relates strongly to the child's environment. "Curiosity grows from the safe and familiar. A secure child with a familiar teacher on a field trip to the zoo will be excited. She will explore and ask dozens of questions," notes scholastic researcher Dr. Bruce Perry.[7] Conversely, the same child may feel threatened and clam up on a trip to the zoo with an unfamiliar teacher. These states are commonly expressed as psychological and physical safety—and there is certainly a message here for how we construct our company and nonprofit cultures to encourage curiosity.

Environments Conducive to Curiosity

Curiosity is a powerful driver of creativity. Walt Disney, the genius who founded the eponymous Walt Disney Corporation, called curiosity the

CURIOSITY AND CONFIDENCE

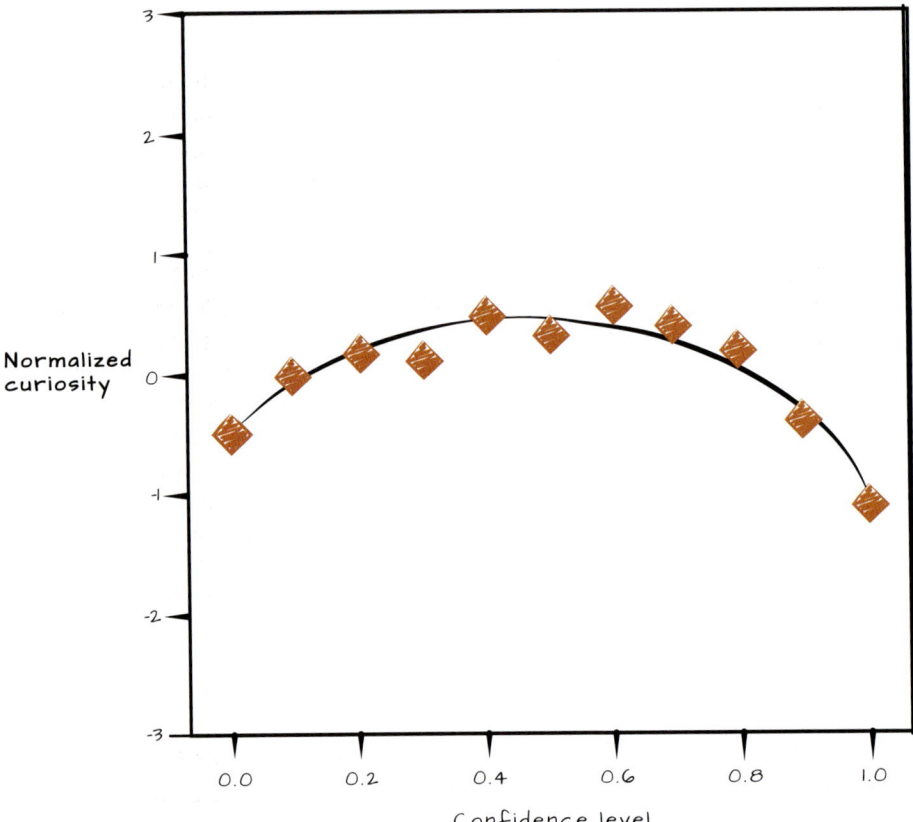

Exhibit 1.1

driving force behind his company's evolution.[8] But many large organizations seem almost hostile to curiosity. Writing in the *Harvard Business Review*, Professor Francesco Gino surveyed 3,000 employees and found that only 24% feel curious in their jobs, compared to 70% who report that they face barriers to asking more questions at work.[9] We understand why companies might be resistant to curiosity—we, too, come from a world of Gantt charts and task lists, project managers, key performance metrics, and hard deadlines. Curious questions can be irritating when you're under pressure. But when companies stifle curiosity, they are shutting off opportunities to search, question, and experiment.

Dedicated Time for Curiosity

Minnesota Mining and Manufacturing, known as 3M, was a pioneer of employee curiosity. In the 1970s the company required employees to dedicate up to 15% of paid hours to noncore projects, in effect challenging them to be curious. Google picked up that idea in 2004 when its founders wrote:

> "We encourage our employees, in addition to their regular projects, to spend 20% of their time working on what they think will most benefit Google. This empowers them to be more creative and innovative. Many of our significant advances happened in this manner."

Even in organizations like Google, though, the pressure of meeting short-term performance targets can gobble up the free time, leading to what has been referred to as "120 percent time."[10] The Alphabet (Google's parent company) policy remains in place, with guidelines that current projects should only consume 80% of employee time. An Alphabet team leader expressed it this way: "It's really not about asking permission for everything you work on—but to empower you to try and experiment—it doesn't have to be a 'moonshot'—just something different."

We are not surprised by the findings of Professor Gino's survey and others like it. These days we all have too little time to daydream and wonder. We know that most profound questions can't be fed into Google, yet "ask Google" has become pervasive shorthand for the idea that all that is known can be found on the web. This blunts and dulls our natural instinct to wonder *why* and *how*. Why think, when you have search engines to find the "answers"? In our grooved or channeled lives, levering ourselves into a place where curiosity and problem solving can thrive requires a huge effort.

Unleashing Curiosity

The research about curiosity is a great starting point for thinking about how to unleash it in organizations. There are three important threads: being in the flow of ideas, asking audacious questions, and recognizing the important contribution that novelty, gestation, and safety play in curiosity-driven problem solving. Exhibit 1.2 takes each of these in turn and shows how individuals from several domains of human endeavor—business, music, and science—have turned curiosity to their and society's advantage.

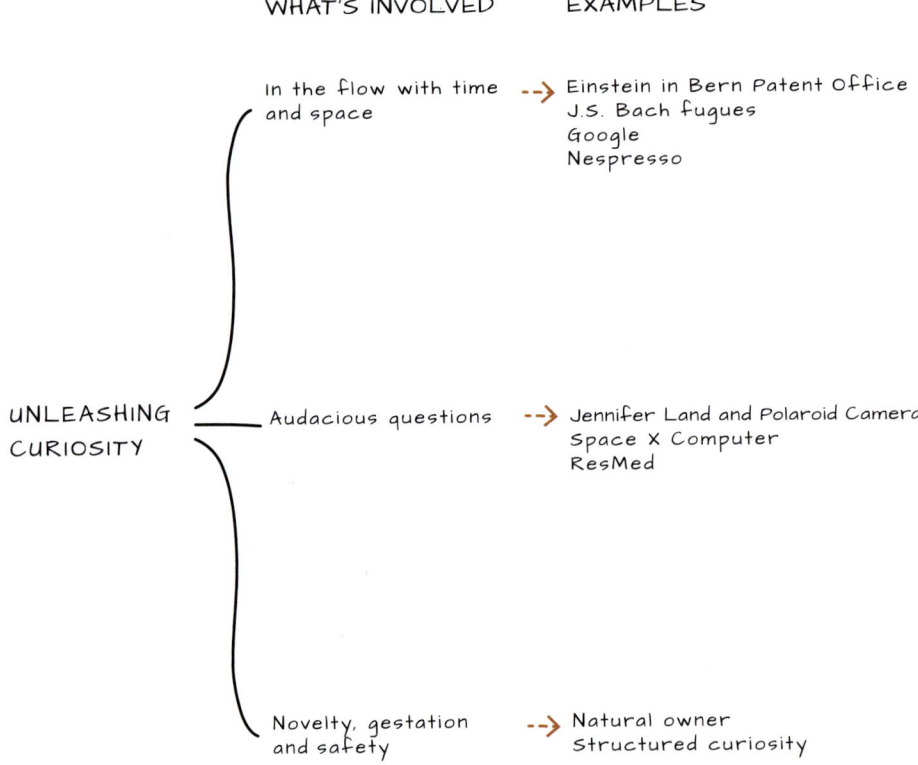

WHAT'S INVOLVED   EXAMPLES

In the flow with time --> Einstein in Bern Patent Office
and space   J.S. Bach fugues
                           Google
                           Nespresso

UNLEASHING   Audacious questions   --> Jennifer Land and Polaroid Camera
CURIOSITY   Space X Computer
                                            ResMed

Novelty, gestation   --> Natural owner
and safety   Structured curiosity

Exhibit 1.2

Flourishing in the Flow of Ideas

Einstein the Patent Clerk

Albert Einstein attributed his genius to curiosity. He famously said, "I have no special talent. I am only passionately curious." We'd venture to suggest that intellectual horsepower had something to do with his success as well. But there was more to Einstein's revolutionary breakthroughs than "just" brainpower and curiosity. He had the great good fortune to be a patent clerk in Bern, Switzerland.

On the face of it, it seems unlikely that a patent clerk in a mid-tier European city should have inspired the greatest innovations in physics for centuries. Einstein took on the role because he hadn't been able to get a teaching position after graduating from the Swiss Federal Polytechnic School two years earlier. A friend of his father eventually offered him a job as technical expert—*third class*—in the Bern patent office in 1902. Einstein was given the responsibilities of reviewing electromagnetic patent applications, making sure they were original, and recommending whether or not an invention warranted a patent. He would do this for seven years. Rather than viewing his lot as lowly and bureaucratic, as many might have done, Einstein described the patent office as his "worldly cloister" where he "hatched his most beautiful ideas."[11] Just three years into this role, in 1905 he published four papers, including one on "special relativity based on the notion of time being relative to the motion of an observer, assuming constant speed of light." Our understanding of physics has never been the same.

Bern in 1902 was what today we would call an innovation hotspot, particularly for electromechanical and electromagnetic devices. From 1902 to 1905 the patent office registered hundreds of relevant patents of impressive range and depth, everything from remote alarms and clocks for railroad departures and arrivals to clocks indicating time in other time zones.[12] The synchronization of time and clocks was a critical challenge for European railroads at the time, particularly for scheduling trains and avoiding accidents on single tracks. Physicist and historian Peter Galison describes the vibrancy of Einstein's inventiveness:

"Patents now raced through the system, improving the electrical pendula, altering the receivers, and expanding system capacity. Time coordination in the central Europe of 1902–1905 was no arcane subject; it was front and center for the clock industry, the military, and the railroad as well as a symbol of the interconnected, sped-up world of modernity. By addressing the problem of distant simultaneity, Einstein was engaging a powerful and highly visible new technology that conventionalized simultaneity, first to synchronize train lines, and to set longitude, and then to fix time zones."

In Galison's view, "time synchronization was the final, crowning step in the development of special relativity."[13]

In today's parlance we might say that Einstein put himself squarely in the flow of ideas, raising the likelihood of insight and discovery. In many ways, the Bern patent office in 1905 was like NASA in the 1960s, or Silicon Valley from the 1970s. It was a remarkable environment for the 26-year-old scientist—a "patent-officer-scientist refracting the underlying metaphysics of his relativity theory through some of the most symbolized mechanisms of modernity."[14]

Time and Space for J.S. Bach

The first piece of classical music Rob recalls hearing as a boy growing up in Broken Hill, Australia, was J.S. Bach's "Jesu, Joy of Man's Desiring." This stunningly beautiful and peaceful composition used to come on the radio at 4 o'clock each afternoon to introduce "The Hospital Hour." It was written in 1723, when Bach took up the position of cantor at St. Thomas's church in Leipzig, Germany, a busy role in which he taught students, composed weekly cantatas, and directed 60 other performances of his own work a year, including festivals.

Bach's life was defined by a tension. Writing music every week "for next Sunday" often got in the way of producing the enduring musical masterpieces for which he is best known. As a result, he went through phases of being weary of his *kapellmeister* responsibilities, notably leading the choir and orchestra. Musicologists have speculated that he eventually became tired of his workload, depressed and burnt out.[15]

It was only when he retired, ending his daily grind, that Bach moved on from church music to produce *The Musical Offering*, *The Goldberg Variations*, and *The Art of Fugue*, none of which he was paid to write.[16] He became curious about how far he could push the boundaries of contrapuntal music—multiple independent melodies, all derived from a 12-note melody. The composition, *Die Kunst Die Fugue*, comprises 14 fugues. It was incomplete at the time of his death, deliberately unfinished, some believe, as a challenge to future generations to write their own ending.[17]

The time and space offered to Bach in retirement allowed him to indulge his curiosity. "Music asked questions of questions."[18] It is no coincidence in our view that much of his music "for next Sunday" has slipped into the annals of history, while his later compositions continue to be performed.

Deep Work to Make a Great Coffee

You have most likely heard of Nespresso, the brand that sells 14 billion coffee capsules each year. You may not have heard of Eric Favre, the person responsible for inventing it. Eric's "deep work" to make a great coffee started in 1973, when he joined Nestlé as an "intrapreneur." But his previous experience, studying thermodynamics and the dynamics of air as a rocket scientist in Switzerland, turned out to be hugely important in the innovation's development.

Eric's challenge was to come up with a better product than Nestlé's two market-leading offerings of the time—the roast and ground coffee prepared in a cafetière or Bialetti on a stovetop, and the soluble Nescafé instant coffee. Full credit should go to the Swiss multinational, a global leader in fast-moving consumer goods, for providing an environment in which Eric could not only indulge his curiosity, but come up with an innovative product that would likely cannibalize its revenues. Nestlé gave him space and time, in his own lab, free of operational demands and of budgetary pressures.

On a visit to Rome with his Italian wife Anna-Maria in the summer of 1975, Eric noticed that some locals were more interested in the quality of the coffee used in their espressos than in the interior design or location of the coffee shop. Curious about this, he discovered Sant'Eustachio II Caffe, steps away from the Piazza Navona. It wasn't much to look at, but he had to queue to get inside. The drinking experience was noticeably different: The coffee was denser, with greater aromas and a distinctive thick "crema" on top. Eric asked to meet the barista, who introduced himself as Eugenio.

Later, Eric set out to make Eugenio's coffee himself, but discovered it wasn't the same. How hard could it be for a rocket scientist to make a cup of coffee? Pretty hard, it turned out. Eric had to concede that it wasn't the espresso machine, the coffee, or the water that made for an otherworldly flavor. It was actually Eugenio himself, with his unique waltz, using an old piston espresso machine, a veritable "chef d'orchestre." But *why* was Eugenio's coffee so much better? Thanks to Anna-Maria's linguistic skills, she and Eric learned about how Eugenio's continuously raising and lowering the lever on his machine affected the brew. While Eugenio believed that his ancient machine was faulty, his stop-and-start actions were inadvertently sucking in more air, compressing it, and injecting it into the capsule. This was the secret that allowed Eric Favre to invent Nespresso (see Exhibit 1.3).

Eric returned to Switzerland, where he had his Eureka moment on a "calm Saturday night dressed in his bathing robe listening to classical music." He went straight to his lab, eager to test his hypothesis. There he had assembled an amalgamation of tubes and cylinders, a filter, ground coffee, hot water, and, most importantly, pressurized air at 200 Bar.

After opening the valve in the way of Eugenio, Eric produced a version of the tasty Sant'Eustachio II Caffe quality crema. True, it was still not up to the standard of the real thing, but it was a crema nonetheless. Eric's

THE DEVELOPMENT OF THE NESPRESSO CAPSULE
ERIC FAVRE'S ORIGINAL EXPERIMENT

Exhibit 1.3
SOURCE: SIMON ALDOUS

curiosity revealed that the key to a perfect espresso could be expressed in a formula:

$$\text{Crema}\left(\text{froth}\right) = \text{Air pressure} + \text{Water} + \text{Coffee}$$

As he dug deeper, he came to understand the true importance of air in the equation, and in particular the importance of the 20% oxygen. The problem had been hard to crack but it was no surprise that the man solving it was an engineer well versed in the dynamics of air.

Nestlé patented the Nespresso system in 1976, and brought it to market 10 years later; in 2021 Nespresso accounted for more than $7 billion in sales for Nestlé. The product's development illustrates the benefits of having time and space to explore curiosity, the resources to experiment, and a charter to innovate and possibly cannibalize a core business.

Audacious Questions

ResMed's Big Questions

We saw at the beginning of this chapter how Jennifer Land's disarming question prompted her father to pursue the goal of an instant camera. Many successful companies would not exist but for relentless curiosity of this sort. One of our favorite examples is ResMed, now a $30 billion leader in the treatment of obstructive sleep apnea (OSA). ResMed was founded by Dr. Peter Farrell, a biomedical engineer who, as vice president of development for Baxter Labs, was looking for new med tech ventures in the mid-1980s. Peter was intrigued when he heard about a sleep treatment, developed by Sydney University's Professor Colin Sullivan, that required patients to wear a fitted mask providing continuous positive airway pressure (later called CPAP). In its first iterations the device made its users look like the Star Wars character Darth Vader, but the idea was revolutionary.[19]

Professor Sullivan's curiosity about sleep had tragically authentic origins: While he was still in medical school, he found his own mother dead in her bed. A long-time snorer, she suffered from a raft of cardiac disorders related to being overweight and a poor sleeper; she had died of a heart attack. As a consequence, Professor Sullivan devoted himself to developing treatments for sleep disorders. "The deep sense of loss and helplessness that, as someone training in medicine, I could not have prevented this in some way, still resonates today."[20]

One patient Professor Sullivan introduced to Peter had sleep issues so severe that he would stop breathing multiple times per hour at night, and inevitably fall asleep during the day. The patient had just had his first rapid eye movement (REM) sleep in years, wearing one of the face masks connected to an 80-pound Hitachi vacuum blower that ran through a wall to his garage. Peter, who says the contraption sounded like a freight train at this stage, assembled a design team to commercialize an integrated mask and machine that was lighter and quieter, and therefore more patient friendly, for home use.

In 1988 the first commercial sales of the Sullivan Nasal CPAP System (R2) were made. The following year Peter bought the business from Baxter and established ResMed to tackle what he viewed as a global market opportunity. He was right. Sullivan had thought that just 2% of the adult population suffered from OSA. More recent data has established that almost 40% of the adult population has a moderate to severe condition. Thanks to the CPAP machine, many sufferers have enjoyed better health and less interrupted nights.

A less curious person might have been tempted to declare victory and take a nap. But Peter was insatiably curious, particularly about whether the CPAP discovery could be associated with more sleep-related health problems. Digging into National Institutes of Health library data, he found that sleep apnea was also the leading cause of high blood pressure. Eventually Peter's curiosity drove a wealth of research, and unlocked discoveries about the links between sleep and strokes, heart disease, and diabetes. Sleep turns out to be the cornerstone of good health, and with the curiosity of Colin Sullivan and Peter Farrell, we now have a clear solution for large populations.

Killer Questions at Space X

There is a special class of curious questions we call "killer questions." These are the questions that cut through stale debates and allow us to see problems from a fresh perspective. They get to the nub of an issue, often in a strikingly blunt way. We know of no script that guarantees killer questions. But we do see a version of the 80:20 rule at work here—5% of team members tend to ask 95% of the killer questions.

> "The best way to manage is to ask questions and not tell people. You can almost always take a directive and turn it into a question. A question shows respect for the person and also engages them in a more thoughtful way. A question means they have to reason on their own and gives them an opportunity to reply if they disagree. You are much better off asking questions, even if you know the answer as a leader. There are urgent cases where you have to state what you want unequivocally, and there are times where consensus does not work. But questions should be the majority of the way you work as a true leader."[22] —Eric Schmidt, former CEO and chair of Google

When Elon Musk interviewed astronomical computer expert Kevin Watson for a role at Space X in 2008, Musk asked if Watson could design a mission-critical computer for $10,000. Kevin Watson may not have used the term "killer question," but he knew it was a big one. To anyone in the aerospace industry it was an insane question: Musk was asking for a computer costing 1/100th of the typical cost of a NASA computer ($10 million). As Watson noted: "In traditional aerospace it would cost you more than ten thousand dollars just for the food at a meeting to discuss the cost of the avionics."[21] With 24 years at NASA, he knew the level of the challenge. Notwithstanding his skepticism, Watson promised Musk that he could deliver on that audacious goal . . . and he did so in less than a year.

Novelty, Gestation, and Safety

Grooved processes, like the regularity of standard operating and strategic planning, together with hierarchy, are the bedrock of organizations, corporate and nonprofit. We need regular processes to coordinate the rhythm and discipline required to run large organizations effectively. But grooved processes and chain of command frequently combine to crowd out curiosity. One way to tackle the impact of these forces on curiosity is to recognize the roles of novelty, gestation, and safety on creativity, and to use them as a counterweight to standard practices and authority.

Novelty and Surprise

From research into child behavior, we know that novelty and surprise play a role in promoting curiosity, which in turn helps take us out of our comfort zone. The child going to the zoo has questions because the experience is novel, and of course because the monkeys inevitably bring surprise and delight with their antics. Teachers understand this and employ it to good effect.

How can this be part of organization life? One way to "skip the needle" is to have major customers come to a board strategy retreat, or to visit an innovation hub where you will likely meet the very tech disruptors looking to eat your lunch. Another is to take a page out of the playbook of the CEO who spent an hour each week donning a headset in the call center, resolving customer issues. There is panic when a CEO or senior executive just turns up at a branch because they are in the neighborhood. In our experience such events are remembered as visits of unusual frankness and candor, when questions are exchanged by the CEO and staff in an open manner. Novelty and surprise also play a key role in convincing people to change, a topic we explore in the show-and-tell mindset chapter.

Quiescent Curiosity

Quiescent curiosity, or latent curiosity, goes hand in hand with deep work. It's the mental process of mulling over problems, putting them away, having them stew half-consciously, only to revisit them when a new situation triggers an insight. Some years ago, Rob and colleague John Stuckey were working with conglomerate businesses and had to answer a fundamental question on corporate strategy: "What businesses should be in our portfolio?" The prevailing wisdom was to adopt the General Electric mantra of being #1 or #2 in market share in an industry, or to exit that business. The concern they had was that in some industries like airlines you could be #1 or #2 and still lose shareholder value. John had leveraged the Structure-Conduct-Performance model to explain this conundrum (in some unattractive industries, industry structure and competitive conduct don't lead to cost of capital returns), but still didn't have an answer to how to decide on the ideal portfolio of businesses.

Rob and John kept wrestling with this problem for a good five years. Their curiosity trigger came during the battles between the financial raiders like T. Boone Pickens and Carl Icahn and established corporates in the 1980s. This led to the insight that the right strategy was to hold a business if you are the "natural owner"—the owner who can generate the largest net present value of cash flows, including options, relative to other competitors.

John was serving a conglomerate with businesses that included tug boats, engineering firms, and coal mines and was trying to advise which businesses to retain and which to divest. Rob was serving a conglomerate with building materials, forestry, and fishing businesses. The natural owner concept introduced a higher bar for deciding what should remain or be added to the portfolio than the conventional "cash flows exceeding acquisition price" test. The term was quickly understood by clients.

CURIOSITY PROMOTERS VS. KILLERS

THIS "Curiosity Promoter"	NOT THIS "Curiosity Killer"
1. Safe environment for questions	"That's a dumb question"
2. Learning from failure	No tolerance for failure
3. Time and space	Current operations 100% +
4. Permitting deep work	Distractions, fragmented time
5. Threats to success	Status quo comfort
6. In the flow of ideas	Internal focus
7. Novelty and surprise	Grooved processes

Exhibit 1.4

The notion of the natural owner, sometimes called the best owner, has been deemed the fourth cornerstone of corporate finance by Tim Koller, co-author of *Value: The Four Cornerstones of Corporate Finance*. The concept was the product of quiescent curiosity triggered by disruptive events in financial markets.

Safety and Creativity

We saw how a child clams up if they consider a trip to the zoo as feeling unsafe. By the same token, having a psychologically safe environment in which to ask "dumb questions" is essential to the promotion of curiosity in organizations. The most inspiring and effective team leaders *speak last* in brainstorming sessions to encourage team members to ask questions and present their views candidly. It's often the most junior member of the team who asks the killer question.

Our friend Professor Robert Wood created the idea of "structured curiosity" to address the issue of psychological safety: Questions not requiring an immediate answer are accumulated and shared at the end of the week in a separate session, without reference to who asked them.[23] He came up with this approach to help his daughter, a junior employee who had been asked by a more experienced colleague, "Why would you ask that?"

Bob reasons that it's difficult to find the best time to ask questions, so having a "parking lot" makes sense to provide that sense of safety. It's worked well and is now being trialed, with his help, at a major bank. See Exhibit 1.4 for a list of curiosity killers and promoters.

Building Curiosity in Your Organization

A former colleague of Rob and Charles heads recruiting for a sizable international consulting firm. He told Rob that his recruiting criteria when interviewing graduates are curiosity, tolerance for ambiguity, and humility, and he has cases to test each attribute. The approach seems to have worked for his firm, but in other organizations merely recruiting for curiosity may not be enough; more comprehensive initiatives may be required. The first step in developing them is to calibrate where you, your team, and your organization really stand on curiosity. Then consider these practical steps to try to make it a feature of "the way we do things around here."

1. *Set a curiosity benchmark.* We all want to know how we compare to others. Dr. Diane Hamilton, author of *Cracking the Curiosity Code,* has developed a curiosity index for this purpose.[24] The index is calculated from an assessment of four curiosity inhibitors, which she calls FATE: fear, assumptions, technology, and environment. By replicating Francesco Gino's survey, then dividing the percentage of respondents who feel curiosity is valued by the percentage who are discouraged

from asking questions, it is possible to derive a rough curiosity quotient (call it CQ). In her survey, it was 24/70, or 34%, across participants. That's a failing grade in our view!

2. *Ask what a good balance between questions and answers looks like.* There is no one fixed balance that applies for all units and seasons. But executives can lay out performance and growth objectives and then map questions and answers against them. We know that organizations that always value answers over questions are likely to fail to innovate, especially in uncertain times.

3. *Introduce structured curiosity.* One useful practice is to set team norms, particularly when deploying teams that are engaged in rapid prototyping for innovation. Agree on what curiosity promoters and killers need to change in order for ambitious objectives to be met. Keep a running log of questions, without attribution, to be addressed at the end of the week.

4. *Make curiosity fun with surprise, novelty, and the joy of child-like questioning.* "Be more curious—damn it!" is unlikely to bring the desired results. You can't just demand curiosity. More curiosity is likely if we put in place the same curiosity triggers that inspire children to ask questions. Step outside regular routines: Encourage mixing across your whole ecosystem (customers, suppliers, technology partners); place a board member into a strategic gaming workshop; ask executive committee members to spend the first hour of their monthly meeting as customer service representatives. Use surprise to get curiosity flowing.

5. *Put yourself in the flow of ideas, do deep work with few distractions, and assess the results.* You don't have to wait for a curiosity policy to emerge in your company. When you embark on your next innovation project, do what Einstein did and put yourself in the flow of ideas. Experiment in a structured way, as Eric Favre did when making Nespresso crema. Negotiate the time and resources to do deep work with minimal distractions. Take stock of the results, and see how your experiment might be extended to other teams. Create a curiosity portfolio of initiatives that you test over time.

Chapter 2
Dragonfly Eye

A New Lens on Recidivism

For millennia, human beings have been wrestling with the twin challenges of crime and punishment. Ancient Sumerians in Mesopotamia wrote the oldest surviving law code about 5,000 years ago—but when they took stylus to tablet, the justice they meted out was pretty rough.[1] Robbery was a capital offense, for instance, so the law enforcers of the day didn't have to worry much about dealing with repeat offenders, also called recidivists. Recidivism became a problem for the United Kingdom around the time of the Industrial Revolution when capital punishment was abolished for many minor crimes, and numbers continued to swell, especially after the practice of sending convicts to penal colonies came to an end (the last prison ship sailed for Australia in 1868).

Experts in criminology and social reformers have long sought to reduce recidivism rates, but they have had little sustained success. Even when they come up with innovative correctional approaches, there remains the challenge of testing them and paying for them. Then one morning in 2010, two young social finance professionals came to the London office of investor Sir Ronald (Ronnie) Cohen. Although Ronnie was a storied pioneer of the British venture capital industry, he had no formal training in criminology. Some years earlier the UK Treasury had invited him to chair a task force on social investment, and with the insights gained from that experience he co-founded Social Finance UK in 2007 to develop new and better ways of tackling social issues around the world. The two executives who came to Ronnie's office that morning explained that they had been working on the issue of prisoners reoffending. "What do you think," they asked, "if we tie a reduction in the number of young people going back to jail to a financial return?"

Ronnie recounts:

"I immediately saw this through the lens of my venture capital career. I opened my eyes wide and said to them, "you have found the key to the capital markets for social entrepreneurs! Let us develop this into an investment product." My experience in VC allowed me to see the opportunity to shape it as a five- to seven-year security".[2]

Recidivism is costly to society. At that time (2010), a shocking three in five of the prisoners released each year from British prisons went on to commit another crime within 18 months, and on average they spent another four months behind bars at an annual expense of £45,000 per prisoner, a cost of billions to the public purse. Something needed to be done. Ronnie needed the British government's support, which quickly came in the shape of an enthusiastic endorsement from then–Justice Minister Jack Straw. "I know we should never do anything for the first time, but we are going to do this," Straw told officials when he heard Ronnie outline the idea.[3]

And so was born the social impact bond (SIB), which became known as the Peterborough bond after the UK prison where the experiment with prisoners first took place. As a financial instrument that shifted the risk of reoffending criminals to the private sector, the bond's key attraction to government decision makers was that returns were tied to results achieved by the program, that is, the reduction in repeat offenses.

Investors committed £5 million to the bond, which offered an annual return of up to 3.5% provided reoffending fell by more than 7.5% across different prisoner cohorts, compared to average figures across the prison system. The challenge of making it happen was handed to charities such as the One Service Program, which worked with prisoners to try to break the cycle.

By any standard the results have been impressive. Ultimately, investors received their capital back with a 3.1% annual return—a decent payback for a government-backed bond. (By comparison, as of late June 2022, the average AAA corporate bond return was about 4%, and the average US tax-free municipal bond returned approximately 3%). If we take a wider societal view, the case is even more compelling, with the substantial reduction in reoffending over the term of the Peterborough bond verified by the not-for-profit independent research institute RAND Europe.[4] Moreover, the UK SIB experience is now being widely applied to tackle other problems across the world: Investors have supported more than 200 SIBs in 35 countries to the tune of about $500 million, addressing social and environmental issues ranging from reducing homelessness to improving early childhood outcomes.[5] To date, SIBs have inspired more than $1 trillion of sustainability-linked bonds and loans—all that as a result of taking a look at a long-standing criminal justice conundrum through a radically different lens.

Seeing Like a Dragonfly

We call this ability to see problems through multiple perspectives or lenses the Dragonfly Eye mindset. The name is inspired by one of the wonders of the natural world, dragonflies. These are not only beautiful creatures, but they have two giant compound eyes with 30,000 lenses or facets, and three further eyes with simple lenses (see Exhibit 2.1) that allow them to see in every direction with almost no blind spots. Their color vision surpasses anything in the insect and animal world.

Exhibit 2.1
SOURCE: MARK MORGAN, FLICKR, CREATIVE COMMONS LICENSE 2.0.

The Dragonfly Eye mindset encourages problem solvers to use a different lens from the one with which they might initially feel comfortable to widen the area that they see, or to zoom in and focus on a key detail. Dan Gardner and Philip Tetlock drew our attention to the image with their description of superforecasters.[6] They observed that superforecasters—individuals who consistently outperform others, including professionals, in forecasting—see the world through one lens, then another, and sometimes through a third.

Taking a 360-degree Dragonfly Eye view of potential threats and opportunities offers businesses an advantage over competitors and illuminates innovative new pathways. Failing to take the Dragonfly Eye view, on the other hand, increases the risk of being blindsided by disruptors.

Anchoring Outside

The term we like to use for taking a 360-degree view of a problem is "anchoring outside." Anchoring *inside*, by contrast, is the view from within your own company or organization. Sometimes the inside view is appropriate: when you are under time pressure, for example, or if the choices are limited. However, when solving complex problems in times of high uncertainty, we encourage decision makers to step back, use their Dragonfly Eye, and see their problem from multiple perspectives, including that of an external disruptor. The recent move by Ford Motor Company to separate its electric vehicle (EV) and internal combustion engine (ICE) units, but under the same corporate parent, is a case in point.[7] The new unit can see the EV problem from a different perspective than the old ICE viewpoint.

Anchoring *inside* could have led to a simple either/or choice for Ford: add more EV cars to existing business units, or spin out EVs into a wholly separate business. But anchoring *outside* reveals more nuance. By looking through multiple lenses, decision makers can see that, for all their differences, the EV and ICE businesses will benefit in numerous ways from being under a single corporate umbrella, compared to stand-alone EV competitors. Dealers, for example, will be happier selling both types of vehicle; the synergies obtained from ordering parts from common suppliers will be retained; and the high costs and great uncertainty of extracting Ford from its contractual obligations in a spinoff will be avoided—not to mention the uncertainty of roiled capital markets.

The story of Thermomix, a kitchen appliance developed by the German conglomerate Vorwerk in the 1960s, provides another example of anchoring outside, in this case in an intensely customer-focused lens. Before embarking on a design, managers contacted French culinary artists with a view to learning how they went about making dishes like thick soups. Team leaders assembled chefs, sous chefs, and assistants, all with different tasks, and carefully studied their preparation routines. In the language of design thinking, the chefs' "pain points" became clear: hand chopping, mincing, frequent stirring to avoid crusting, and pureeing. All these perspectives were effectively different mini-customer lenses, vital to the process of innovation. By tapping into the chefs' deep understanding, the company was able to produce the world's most versatile kitchen appliance—one that saves up to 50% of chopping and prepping time. It weighs, chops, grates, stirs, cooks, purees, mills, kneads, juices, makes sorbet and ice cream, and steams fish and vegetables in a single device. Today's Thermomix is used by millions of chefs and home cooks around the world.

A Perspective from Japanese Management

Decision makers can develop a 360-degree outside view of the business landscape by mapping the ecosystems of customers, suppliers, competitors, regulators, and disrupters. In this regard they can take inspiration from the way that many business meetings are conducted in Japan, with each participant typically asked to provide neutral information from their perspective. In the West, by contrast, business managers are more likely to set out an argument favoring their particular perspective and hope that it will prevail. The Japanese managers seek to create the neutral map first, which may result in it being richer and more detailed. The assumption is that when the map is finished, the appropriate course becomes obvious to everyone.[8]

Framing the Dragonfly Eye

Too often managers rely on a single lens to look at problems. Examples of a single lens view include an exclusive focus on market share, net promoter score, or the ratio of long-term customer value (LTV) to customer acquisition cost (CAC). A single lens may be a helpful simplifier but risks oversimplification and myopia in its use.

We like to think of the Dragonfly Eye mindset in three sets of actions: changing the lens or perspective, widening the aperture, and seeing the problem through multiple perspectives (see Exhibit 2.2). Let's look at some examples of each of these.

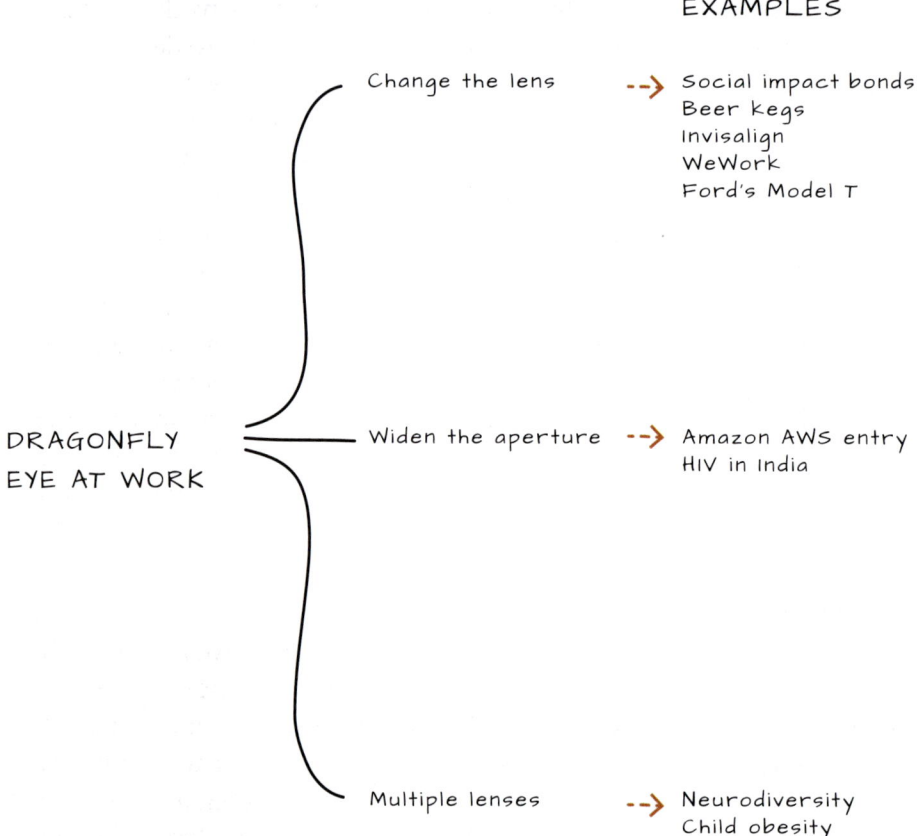

EXAMPLES

Change the lens --> Social impact bonds
Beer kegs
Invisalign
WeWork
Ford's Model T

DRAGONFLY
EYE AT WORK — Widen the aperture --> Amazon AWS entry
HIV in India

Multiple lenses --> Neurodiversity
Child obesity

Exhibit 2.2

The Power of Changing Lenses

Beer Kegs as Technology

Radically changing competitive landscapes with constant threat of disruption are becoming the new normal. "Every company is a technology company" is how strategist and former McKinsey colleague Chris Bradley expresses it.[9] Players *external* to an industry are often in the forefront of reimagining it, bringing a different lens to those used by incumbents. Continuing to use a lens that has worked well in the past is a risky way to head off the threat of radical change. For the same reasons, employing an objectives and key results (OKR) dashboard built around a legacy perspective may be perilous.

Consider beer kegs. Traditionally, a beer company owns the kegs and sells the brew to customers; it has a weekly order pattern to deliver full kegs and collect the empty ones. For decades that was how the market worked, but in 2019 a group of entrepreneurs injected new froth into beverage logistics with a start-up called Konvoy.[10] By applying a technology company lens to the problem, Konvoy developed a "smart keg" with a passive tracking beacon and a software system to identify the location of kegs and the temperature of the beer. Using the Internet of things (IoT), small packets of data are emitted from the keg on the zero G network, allowing bar owners and beer producers to analyze purchase patterns and replenish stock levels more efficiently. Keg inventory turnover has increased from four to five times per annum, and makers of unpasteurized beer, who traditionally face losses when beer temperatures increase, now have a tool that allows them to proactively reduce product wastage. Even beer kegs are tech now.

A Fresh Look at Braces

For years, orthodontics conjured up one not very attractive image: bright hard metal braces on teenage teeth. Archaeological evidence from excavated mummies suggests that some Egyptians in the time of the Pharaohs had metal posts affixed to their teeth with a catgut cord that presumably shifted their incisors into alignment.[11] These ancient techniques were not totally unlike the ones used to straighten teeth with metal braces for most of the twentieth century. Although modern dentists also utilize rubber bands and spacers, the classic bracket-and-wire construction had remained largely unchanged.

Then, in the 1990s, Kelsey Wirth and Zia Chishti, MBA students at Stanford Business School with no qualifications in dentistry, worked to apply a fresh and different lens to orthodontics.[12] Zia only had the financial means to correct his teeth as an adult, shortly before business school, which was awkward and embarrassing for him. When he finally got his braces off, he noticed two important things. First, his retainer was almost invisible, and second, it still moved his teeth if he forgot to wear it for a few days. This small insight inspired a revolutionary hypothesis: If a simple plastic retainer could move teeth a little, perhaps the technology could be altered and improved to move teeth a lot, but with better curbside appeal than conventional braces. Maybe, in fact, a form of plastic teeth straightener could do away with the need for metal braces altogether. By looking at the problem of straightening teeth through this novel lens, Zia and Kelsey adapted existing aspects of orthodontics to make orthodontic treatment less painful, less embarrassing, and more affordable.

Kelsey and Zia proposed a series of clear, custom-manufactured, removable plastic alignment retainers, created from software-designed treatment plans. They called their solution Invisalign, emphasizing that the aligners would be inconspicuous to the casual observer. By changing to a new set every few weeks, the patient's teeth would gradually move into the desired position without the need for metal braces.

Kelsey and Zia recruited engineers to test the hypothesis that plastic retainers could be designed to straighten teeth. They also contacted orthodontists (cold-calling through the Bay Area phone book) in the hopes of running clinical trials. Initially none of the orthodontists returned their calls. Remember, disruption seldom comes from within! Eventually, Kelsey and Zia entered into a partnership with the dean of the University of Pennsylvania Dental School, a relationship that has been crucial to the success of Invisalign.

Kelsey and Zia found financial backing from Joe Lacob of the venture capital firm Kleiner Perkins, which took the company public on NASDAQ in 2001 with a billion-dollar valuation. Today the company is a market leader in orthodontics, with a market capitalization over $15 billion. New lenses can be powerful.

Choosing the Wrong Lens: WeWork

In our work with organizations, we always start by seeing how the problem looks through a variety of lenses. We look to see which lens provides the most insight in breaking down a complex problem, and then chart a path through uncertainty. This willingness to question what you see through your initial lens is an essential part of the Dragonfly Eye mindset, a critical way of avoiding decision-making biases, particularly availability and confirmation bias. Settling too quickly on the wrong lens can have serious consequences. The classic mistake here is the anology trap, which we believe is at play in the WeWork story.

When decision makers compare the potential growth trajectory of a new product with that of another product that has shown past exponential growth, they risk stumbling into the *analogy trap*. "It's just like the growth profile of Facebook," you hear one entrepreneur say, or, "These projections remind me of the iPhones 1–4." Right. We all love analogies, and done right they can allow teams to gain a quick insight. But an analogy should always be qualified, scrutinized from different angles, and its underlying assumptions tested for genuine comparability. Only then is it possible to draw a realistic conclusion on the explanatory value of the analogy—and to understand the circumstances under which it may break down.

The siren call of exponential growth attracted multiple investors when WeWork, a provider of shared office spaces, looked set to launch an IPO in 2019. Through one lens, WeWork appeared to be an entrepreneur's dream. Like the Facebook app, the iPhone, and the eBay platform, WeWork's growth appeared to be powered by "network effects," a concept popularized by 3Com co-founder Robert Metcalfe. Metcalfe's law says that the value of a network increases to the square of the nodes in the network.[13] A network of 10 nodes has a value of 100 (10×10); an additional node raises the value to 121 (11×11), and one more node raises it to 144. When Charles was CEO of Citysearch, owners of the dating site Match.com, he saw how strong network effects on the site increase the chances of users finding a partner, and therefore each additional user adds a larger increment of value than the previous one. This kind of network effect is also called increasing returns to scale.

WeWork's negative equity in accounting terms at the time of the IPO plan was $2.3 billion. Yet based on the IPO price it was exploring, its imputed market capitalization was a staggering $47 billion. Companies are valued primarily on their expected future cash flows, but that valuation assumed both increasing returns to scale and exponential growth in revenue. Today its market capitalization is less than $2 billion.

The WeWork story is a cautionary tale. The company was backed by Masayoshi Son, founder and chairman of Softbank, and an extraordinarily successful investor in technology companies whose enthusiasm in this case looks almost reckless. "When Masa chose to invest in me for the first time, he only met me for 28 minutes,"[14] according to WeWork founder Adam Neumann.

To be fair to WeWork, its business model—leasing office space from commercial property owners and then providing short-term leases to tech companies in open offices that have social amenities—does have *some* network effects. Its customers, for example, can use multiple WeWork locations within a single city or when visiting a different city. And the operating software and brand marketing across many locations may convey some scale economies. However, Metcalfe's law does not apply. WeWork has few economies of scale in its fundamentals: It needs more physical space as it adds customers, a linear relationship well known to commercial real estate lessors. WeWork valued itself not as a commercial real estate company, but through the lens of a different business model, as a network tech company. As the company put it: "based on the value of our integrated solution-space, community, services and technology—and the scale of our global platform."[15]

WeWork's leaders no doubt sincerely believed that it would grow rapidly with better and better unit economics. Had they tried on the lens from the office leasing industry, however, they might have scaled back their projections. Today, the company's financial reports read more like the real estate leasing company that it really is—highlighting its gross desk sales, revenue, and occupancy levels, which in mid-2022 stood at 66%.

The Force-Fitting Trap

Another related trap for the unwary is to force-fit a lens. Henry Ford famously saw business from the then-novel perspective of mass production and rationalization, a lens that worked for over 15 years with the success of the Model T. In 1909, he famously said that "[a]ny customer can have a car painted any color that he wants so long as it is black."[16] Millions of Model Ts over the following decade and a half proved him right. But as the Roaring Twenties shifted into high gear, consumer needs were evolving and by the end of the decade Model Ts finally stopped rolling off the production line. Ford had fallen into the force-fitting trap. Later he failed again when he mistakenly viewed rubber farming though the lens of mass production, creating the Amazonian jungle city of Fordlandia in Brazil in 1927, with the aim of rationalizing his supply chain. It soon became clear that the production line methods that worked for automobiles would not work for harvesting rubber in the Amazon. His grandson, Henry Ford II, wound up selling the project back to Brazil in 1945 at a massive loss.[17] Henry Ford revolutionized automobile manufacture with the production line and built a great fortune—but then he tried to apply that lens to all that followed. To a man with a good hammer, every problem looks like a nail!

Widening the Aperture

As discussed earlier, we adopt a Dragonfly Eye mindset by anchoring ourselves outside the organization, applying multiple perspectives to the problem from the whole ecosystem. Of course this is not always easy to achieve in practice—we tend to get stuck in our original lenses (think about those gold or blue dress optical illusions, where you just can't see it the other way). As you consider potential moves by customers, suppliers, and competitors, it is critical to understand what you *don't* know, just as much as what you are certain about.

One way to do this is to widen the aperture of your lens. An aperture is an opening; in optics, the wider the aperture, the more light can pass through. A photograph looks different when we widen the aperture. Great problem solvers often widen the aperture by looking at the problem "from 30,000 feet." Dragonflies hovering 10 feet above the ground can see almost every aspect of their predators and prey. The effect can be panoramic—and clarifying—when context and setting are brought together in a zoomed-out perspective.

Amazon's Head Start in Cloud Computing

Today we take cloud computing for granted, but the market didn't even exist a generation ago. The competitive dynamics behind the development of cloud computing have been as intense as they have been rapid. Yet the big competitors did not all line up at the starting line at a single moment. As Amazon Web Services (AWS) CEO Adam Selipsky remarked in 2021, "We got a 5–7-year head start on the competition with our cloud offering."[18] So why was Amazon, initially an online retailer, able to steal a march on tech companies such as Google, Microsoft, and IBM?

The story goes back to the early 2000s, when a range of players approached Amazon wanting to use merchant.com, its ecommerce platform that gave third-party retailers (such as Target) the toolkit to set up their own web stores.[19] Through merchant.com, Amazon had a window on adjacent businesses; it could see other retailers' emerging needs for ecommerce, including storage and analytics. It realized that there was a growing demand for services beyond what would be traditionally categorized as retail. This was not yet cloud computing as we understand it today, but a wider aperture showed Amazon that there might be growth opportunities for itself in the early endeavors of those companies to whom it had opened its platform.

When Jeff Bezos gave Andy Jassy, now Amazon CEO, his first big role in 2002, Jassy's task was to find out why internal projects were taking longer than expected. The problem, he soon discovered, was that there was no central development platform.[20] Jassy therefore decided that Amazon should reconfigure its infrastructure so that different tech teams could share the same software building blocks for their projects. Amazon soon realized that it could also capitalize externally on Jassy's internal work with toolsets like merchant.com.[21] So the company began solving for something Google and Microsoft had not yet clearly envisaged: a customer who used Amazon's internal infrastructure services for its external projects. Amazon executives started toying with the idea of external developers making use of the company's computing and storage infrastructure as well as software building blocks. A new, game-changing business unit was coming into focus.

Jassy took over an existing Amazon division and expanded it with the promise that any enterprise could have access to "the same cost structure and scalability of infrastructure as the largest company in the world."[22] Amazon also directed a website engineering team in South Africa to develop a system called EC2 for centralizing computational power.[23] That technology fitted exactly what Jassy had in mind for AWS. Suddenly, customers could use Amazon's infrastructure in a more flexible way, accessing and applying Amazon's computational power for their own use.

By 2006, Amazon's customers could rent the services for as little as 10 cents an hour, a revolutionary solution that remains the foundation of Amazon cloud computing.[24] Today AWS holds more than 40% of the cloud computing market—its closest competitor holds just 19%.[25] By widening the aperture, Amazon was able to identify an adjacent market opportunity, which it then made its own.

Solving a Health Crisis

In 2002 the Bill & Melinda Gates Foundation asked our former colleague Ashok Alexander to lead the response team in India after a dramatic surge in HIV was threatening to take infections to a level hitherto only seen in Southern Africa.

The answer was not immediately apparent. After digging into the data and receiving briefings from HIV experts, Ashok could see the problem but not the solution. The existing lens was medical, one of pandemic, but this wasn't yielding useful insights. So, using the mindset of a Dragonfly Eye, Ashok widened the aperture. One of the issues he spotted from 30,000 feet was the social dynamics of female sex workers and their customers (a group that encompassed many long-distance truckers), including the need to reduce the violence present in sex work.

By taking this broader perspective, he gave voice to female sex workers—and it was they who helped reduce the crisis. Ashok saw that sex work was not only fueling the HIV upsurge, it could also provide a potential solution. He subsequently met thousands of sex workers in six Indian states where HIV was growing rapidly, questioning them on their clients' use of condoms, explaining that condom negotiation was the key to HIV prevention. The Avahan Program, as it came to be known, was rolled out across the six states in only two years, and is estimated to have prevented 600,000 infections of the deadly disease.[26]

A Multi-Lens Approach

Let's return for a moment to the dragonfly. This flying insect's true beauty is *not* that it possesses so many lenses, but that it can synthesize what it can see from so many of them at once. It combines, as our former colleague Dominic Barton phrased it, "a telescope *and* microscope"—except with many, many more lenses.[27]

When we approach complex problems under conditions of high uncertainty, it's not surprising that a single lens reveals only part of the picture. Author Shane Parrish of the *Farnam Street* blog explains that "most problems are multi-dimensional, and thus having more lenses often offers significant help with the problems we are facing." Parrish goes on to describe the value of multiple lenses in a compelling way:

> *"The more lenses used on a given problem, the more of reality reveals itself. The more of reality we see, the more we understand. The more we understand, the more we know what to do."*[28]

The Neurodiversity Lens and a Digital Twin for Kelp Forests

Lawrence Fung of Stanford's Neurodiversity Project has observed that successful problem solvers in Silicon Valley often show signs of being on the neurodiverse spectrum. Such individuals "have a unique ability to connect the dots, which allows them to reach conclusions quickly. Neurodiverse individuals have cognitive tendencies to look at the details first before the bigger picture, contrary to how most people dissect an issue, essentially broaching an issue from a very different lens or level."[29] Understanding broad patterns and simultaneously being hyperfocused on the detail is an excellent example of bringing a Dragonfly Eye mindset to some of the world's most difficult problems.

Let's look at an example. Seaweed from underwater kelp forests is attracting unprecedented attention at the moment. It holds huge potential as a blue carbon sink, able to absorb more CO_2 than that of comparable forests on land. *Asparagopsis* seaweed, a species of red algae, has the potential to partially eliminate methane from cattle emissions (otherwise known, in less polite company, as cow burps). Kelp forests are found in 48 million square kilometers of the oceans of the world, an area over five times the size of the United States, and they can grow as much as two feet per day.[30]

One novel solution to create new kelp forests on Australia's Great Barrier Reef is to install floating platforms, at a depth of 25 meters, which will harness energy from ocean waves and restore nutrient upwelling to levels recorded before global warming. GeoSynergy, a Geographic Information Systems (GIS) consulting company led by CEO Geoff Osborn, has envisaged a three-dimensional, digital twin of the proposed kelp forest to help model how to build and operate the project. The model would link the physical world of the floating platform with marine permaculture arrays (MPAs) to the digital world, factoring in water temperature cooling and the effects on kelp growth, as well as sensors to pick up CO_2 absorption. Geoff, who has already developed other successful digital twin projects, approaches problem solving with his team both by looking for patterns and by drilling down with an intense focus on discrete elements to see how they affect, and are affected by, other complex elements.

Geoff decided that the best candidate for the kelp forest project was Aiden, a 17-year-old who is neurodiverse (in this case on the autism spectrum) and nonverbal. Aiden is highly knowledgeable about game engines such as Unreal Engine and Fortnite and has contributed to design features. A game engine consists of a rendering engine for handling images, and one for 3D objects, a physics engine, libraries for artificial intelligence, and memory management. Geoff recalls that when he interviewed Aiden the teen displayed the technical maturity of a GIS professional in his mid-30s.

Aiden became convinced that building a kelp forest digital twin "required my skills in computer graphics and experience with Unreal Engine to enable the rendering of a few thousand MPAs . . . and having them all stimulate buoyancy without negatively impacting the performance of the app. A single MPA is represented as a 3D model in Unreal Engine which is instanced across different locations during the simulation. The kelp is a bunch of 2D planes currently animated as a pixel shader."[31]

Not easy to follow, right? That is the point: Aiden has a unique set of capabilities that are a sort of superpower associated with his neurodiversity. In this case they provide a special lens or perspective on an incredibly complex modeling project with a large number of variables.

Obesity and Wicked Problems

Multiple lenses are especially valuable where there is a community or societal dimension. We brought researchers to the team room at Rhodes House in Oxford to explore obesity in developed countries, an extraordinarily complex and challenging problem. These kinds of complex challenges are often defined as "wicked problems" (after a landmark 1970s paper by that title). Wicked problems are those that are hard to get your arms around because they involve multiple and interlocking causes, values disagreements among stakeholders, a need for substantial behavioral change, and often unintended consequences from policy changes.

One way to capture that complexity in the case of obesity is to draw a Foresight Obesity System Map, shown in Exhibit 2.3.[32] The map is a linked diagram of the factors at play, including physical activity, degree of primary appetite control, psychological stress, self-esteem, and other factors. Looking at it, you can easily understand why this is a wicked problem!

Where should researchers start? With this kind of problem, it is literally like unraveling the ball of string that this problem resembles. With

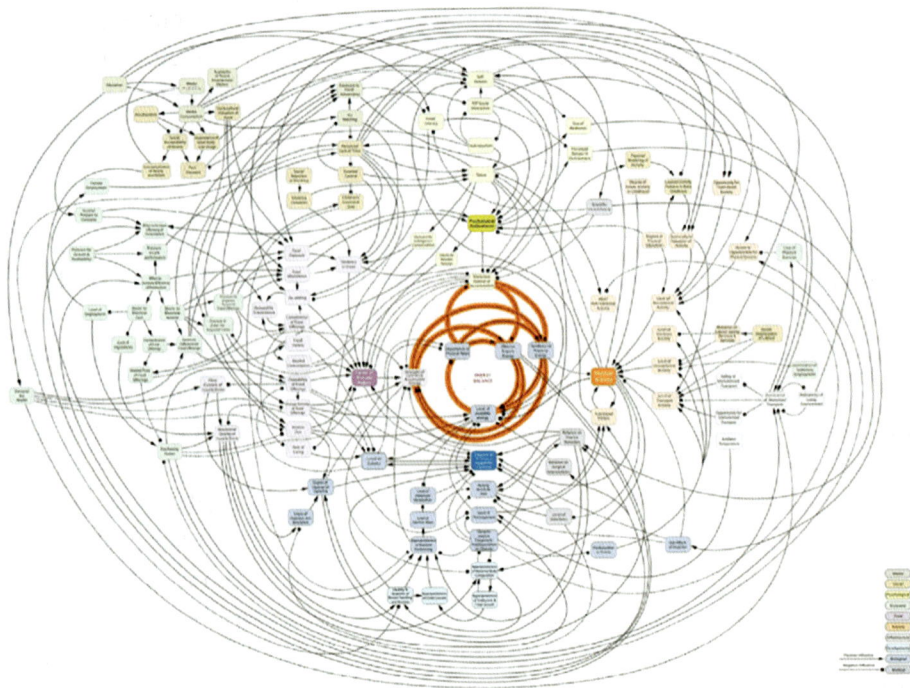

Exhibit 2.3

our Oxford team, we began with a geographic lens: Were there any developed countries that had *low* obesity rates? Japan stood out for its low levels of obesity. We then ran a simple calories in/out comparison of the United States and Japan. In Japan, people both consume fewer calories and expend more of them each day than people in the United States. We sought to understand why the Japanese expend more calories. Our hypothesis was that thanks to the layout of cities Japanese people spend less time in cars and more time walking. This led us to explore walkability as a variable.

Our team tried a number of other lenses, or cleaving frames, such as incentives versus regulation. Using this lens allowed us to explore what happens when regulations are applied, for example, to the advertising and availability of sugary drinks (turns out, not a lot).

We also looked at socioeconomic lenses. Previous research has linked levels of income and education to obesity.[33] One of our researchers set out to test the relationship between obesity and four variables: income, education, walkability, and a climate-based comfort index (temperature and humidity). Using data from 68 cities, the researcher concluded that all four variables were statistically significant and negatively correlated with obesity. A whopping 82% of the variance could be explained by the four variables—that sounds great, but none of those levers are easy to move for most populations.

In addition to socioeconomic factors, we also explored intergenerational effects. Obese mothers are estimated to have a 33% higher risk than their nonobese counterparts of having an obese baby and an obese 6-year-old. Forty percent of obese children become obese adolescents; 75–80% of obese adolescents become obese adults. Viewed this way, it was striking how much might be achieved by starting with the mother-child relationship.

As we talked through our emerging findings with contributors to our first book, *Bulletproof Problem Solving*, we learned that hypotheses about the determinants of child obesity could be tested with novel survey data and modern statistical inference methods. A philanthropic organization, the Paul Ramsay Foundation, expressed interest in funding research by a cross-disciplinary team from the University of Sydney to test the relationship between socioeconomic status and child obesity, and to see if a Bayesian approach could bring new insights. Bayesian statistics are sometimes called conditional probabilities, which are updated as new information comes to light.

The Sydney researchers located a dataset of children and their families' socioeconomic status, education, and body mass index (BMI). Overlaying a Bayesian network design, they were able to see clusters of variables, and isolate whether those variables were causal or simply associated. They displayed the findings in what are called Directed Acyclic Graphs such as the one shown in Exhibit 2.4. There is a prominent link between socioeconomic status, BMI of the primary caregiver, maternal education (specifically whether the mother completed the 12th grade), and the BMI of the child.

The analysis shows the value of bringing multiple lenses to bear on complex problems. Our conclusions don't mean that cities should necessarily add new walkways, or that regulators should rethink their approach to sugary foods. But we do have a new insight in the apparent power of addressing social disadvantage, notably by improving educational opportunities for young women.

DIRECTED ACYCLIC GRAPH - CAUSALITY DIRECTION

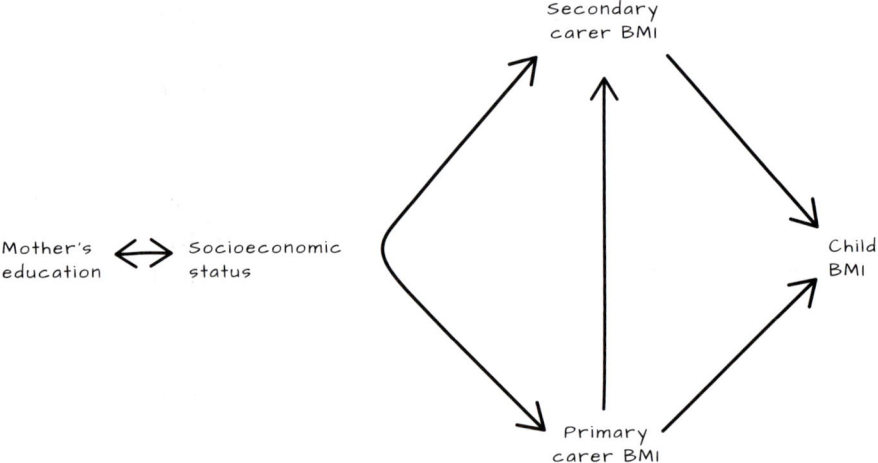

Exhibit 2.4
SOURCE: PROFESSOR SALLY CRIPPS.

Bringing a Dragonfly Eye into Your Organization

Adopting a Dragonfly Eye mindset doesn't require the recruitment of superforecasters or Bayesian statisticians. There is a set of actions every organization can take to apply this strategic mindset to problem solving.

1. *Take stock of the lenses you can use for tackling uncertainty and complex problems.* Are you trying different lenses, and attempting to widen the aperture on the most pressing organizational challenges? Are customer journeys examined, and the results used? Do you use red and blue teams to assess the responses of competitors to your actions? Have you thought about your company as a technology company?
2. *Use analogies as different lenses but subject them to scrutiny for applicability and bias.* When a CEO or other senior manager says "this is just what I came across at my last gig," it takes an open-minded organization to encourage a team member to tease out similarities and differences in the analogy. But it's crucial to avoid the analogy trap.
3. *Assess whether there are barriers to using different lenses or widening the aperture.* It takes time and money to try different lenses on a problem, or widen the aperture, and sometimes there is no immediate

payoff. The Avahan program researchers spent 12 months listening to women and exploring the link between sex work and violence before a solution could be rolled out across India. Have you framed the big issues that warrant using different lenses? Are OKR processes supportive of different lenses? Do your incentive systems make it hard to bring a new lens to the table?

4. *Ask if teams anchor outside and start problem solving with an ecosystem map and a theory of change.* Are key uncertainties about demand evolution or competitor action mapped into the ecosystem view? Are leading-edge customers engaged with you in innovation, like the French chefs who helped develop Thermomix?

5. *Having mapped a complex system with major uncertainty, explore if there are routes to insight via different lenses.* The socioeconomic lens opened a world of insights into the causes of child obesity, particularly when married to different analytic tools like Bayesian networks.

6. *Tailor investment in getting a 360-degree view.* Amazon's AWS is an interesting case in point. Cloud computing in 2005 was only an idea with no guarantee of success—but Andy Jassy's request for 57 staff to launch the venture was a relatively modest one and, had it fizzled, it wasn't going to sink the parent company. Not a bad bet, though, for an enterprise valued at over $500 billion in 2022—more than IBM, Oracle, and SAP combined.

Chapter 3
Occurrent Behavior

Let's Weigh the Money

A story about experimenting on a high-stakes problem for the Federal Reserve Bank has stuck with us for years. Two of our former colleagues, Ted Hall and Don Watters, explain:

> *"We found that there were hundreds of people who worked six-hour shifts (at the Fed) counting money. They would open the packs received from commercial banks and recount them. The frequency of over- or under-counts in those packs was very low."*[1]

Ted and Don considered the costs of this time-consuming approach and asked themselves what the alternatives were. Counting machines were at least a decade away. Then Don had an epiphany: On a visit to San Francisco's Wells Fargo Museum, he recalled seeing the precision scales used for weighing gold during the California Gold Rush, and wondered if the bills in the Federal Reserve could also be weighed with such a device.

Ted and Don decided to conduct an experiment. They set up two bundles of paper currency in the vault, arranging for one to be counted by humans and the other packets to be weighed against the standard weight they had determined. "Then, using statistical sampling, we analyzed which system was more accurate at identifying the overs and unders."

Arthur Burns, chair of the Federal Reserve, was on hand to observe the test and see the results. Initially, both the "piece-verified" pallet (the one that had been counted twice by hand) and the second pallet, which was weighed and statistically sampled, were certified as error-free. As a next step the piece-verifier crew checked the weighed/sampled pallet, and the weighed/sampled crew checked the piece-verified one. The piece-verified pallet turned out to be riddled with errors, while there were no errors at all in the weighed/sampled pallet. "It seems like we have a clear answer," the Fed chair declared, puffing on his ever-present pipe.

Thanks to this experiment the Fed abandoned its traditional way of doing things, moving from a system of hand counting 100% of its packs of bills to not counting them at all. Later, the Comptroller of the Currency rejected the weighing and sampling of larger-denomination bills on the grounds that it would potentially compromise the integrity of the US financial system. Nonetheless, Ted and Don's team had not only improved the accuracy of a high-stakes procedure, but had reduced Fed operating expenses by millions of dollars a year.

Occurrent Behavior and Problem Solving

"Problem solving requires selective trial and error. The more difficult and novel the problem, the greater . . . the amount of trial and error required".
Nobel laureate Herb Simon[2]

Occurrent behavior is a term that describes what actually happens in the world rather than what was modeled or predicted. It is a slightly strange term, but we think it captures an important strategic problem solving mindset, the inclination to run a fresh experiment and generate new data rather than relying on old datasets and conventional answers.

Occurrent behavior is relentless experimenting to reduce uncertainty, via deliberate trial and error of the kind carried out at the Federal Reserve. Using this mindset, great problem solvers constantly test hypotheses. The results help decide their next steps—either to abandon a path, decide with confidence to proceed, or to collect more data to become comfortable making a decision. This mindset involves testing and deliberation, which may be why most organizations are not very good at it: Managers expect instant answers, and their fear of failure or being caught out can outweigh rational risk-taking.

Thinking Like a Bayesian

Today, we take it as common sense that the way to address a problem under uncertainty is to start with what we know, propose an explanation, and then collect data to see whether the evidence supports the hypothesis—and then to update the hypothesis given what we have actually observed. This is the essence of the scientific method: reducing uncertainty by experimenting. It's an approach that was formalized in what has become known as Bayes' rule, after Thomas Bayes, an eighteenth-century statistician and clergyman (see Exhibit 3.1).

BAYES RULE IN ACTION

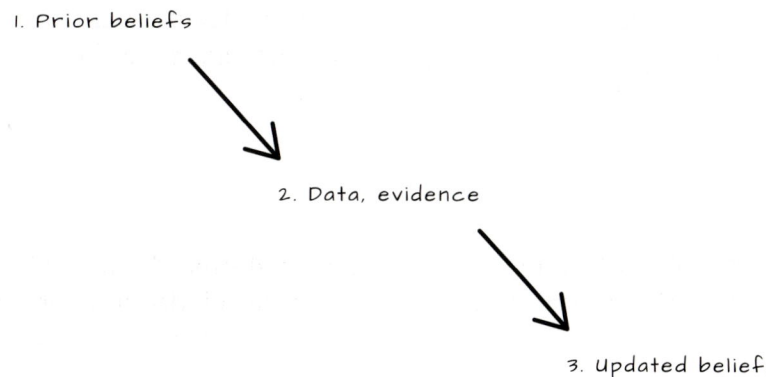

1. Prior beliefs

2. Data, evidence

3. Updated beliefs

Exhibit 3.1

For mathematics buffs, Bayes' rule goes like this:

$$\text{Updated probability}\,(posterior)\,p(\text{Hypothesis}\,/\,\text{Evidence}) =$$
$$p(\text{Hypothesis})(prior) \times p(\text{Evidence}\,/\,\text{Hypothesis})\,/\,p(\text{Evidence})$$

Bayes' rule estimates the probability that a hypothesis is true given the evidence from the data. Consider, for example, car accidents. Who is most likely to cause them? From years of observation, we know that the risk is greater for new drivers. Bayes' rule informs car insurers that they should charge higher premiums for teenage drivers, rather than assign a single premium for everyone based on the broader average probability of accidents for all drivers. It's a dream solution for problem solvers. Little wonder that Bayesian approaches are applied in settings from political polling to actuarial assessment to pharmaceutical trials. Our examples of leaning into risk in the Imperfectionism Mindset chapter also follow a Bayesian approach. And the child obesity case in the Dragonfly Eye Mindset chapter illustrates how formal Bayesian analysis can assist with causality in examining data.

Bayes' rule is the core intellectual scaffolding for the mindset of occurrent behavior. Start with what we have observed, estimate the probability of an occurrence if a hypothesis is true, then update your beliefs as you follow the evidence. When Bayesian adaptive trials are conducted, teams determine the most informative experiment, the one that has the greatest reduction in uncertainty. Thank you, Reverend Thomas Bayes!

Framing Occurrent Behavior

When we were management consultants, we discovered for ourselves that the best way to solve strategic problems is by testing a hypothesis against real experimental evidence. We've also seen the approach go wrong. Too often, junior or less curious senior problem solvers conflate the "hypothesis" they start with as the "solution" and immediately try to prove it. But a hypothesis is most definitely *not* the solution. It must be tested and challenged—or rejected—in the light of what the data actually demonstrate. Time is understandably a constraint; most organizations can't wait for the outcome of multi-year randomized control trials (RCTs). So, we look for experiments that we could conduct in a timely and cost-effective way.

Here are some diverse real-life examples:

- *Trees in New Guinea:* We hypothesized that a forest resource in Papua, New Guinea, had adequate reserves for the future. To prove or disprove the hypothesis, we conducted log tests, and peeled previously untested species for plywood. We discovered there were indeed sustainable species available that could greatly extend the life of sawmills and provide jobs in the community.
- *Beyond the beer hall:* We hypothesized that a pubs business could grow profitably if it were to invest in associated food and liquor outlets. To test that hypothesis, we built a multiple regression model, using data from about 500 pubs, to calculate the added contribution from the new businesses, adjusting for competitors in the neighborhood. The model confirmed our hypothesis. Over time, pubs became food and beverage outlets as much as beer halls.
- *Steel nerves:* We hypothesized that remote steel mills could be competitive despite their location. We found a steel plant at Lulea in the Arctic Circle, 900 kilometers from Stockholm, and calculated the additional costs that could be attributed to its remoteness. We then applied that financial penalty to a remote semi-desert plant in Australia, 400 kilometers from its regional capital, and found that, like its Swedish counterpart, the cost of its remoteness was more than offset by the savings from being so close to iron ore resources. Both plants remain open decades later.

- *Distributing free money:* The city of Stockton, California, which has serious income and employment issues, wanted to test a hypothesis that giving away free money would encourage recipients to work less. In an experiment with an RCT, 125 people received $500 per month for 24 months, while another 125 were matched as the control group. It turned out that rather than wasting the funds, those receiving the income support used the money to find new jobs. In a year, the number of recipients with a full-time job rose from 28 to 40, a 43% increase, compared to a 5% increase for the control group.[3]

Experiments such as these have made us disciples of occurrent behavior. To pursue occurrent behavior we have to do three things (see Exhibit 3.2). First, we look to *create or use data in real time.*

Second, we explore whether there are *new tools or novel ways* to capture and observe existing data, in order to generate insight and reduce uncertainty. And third, we use *natural experiments.*

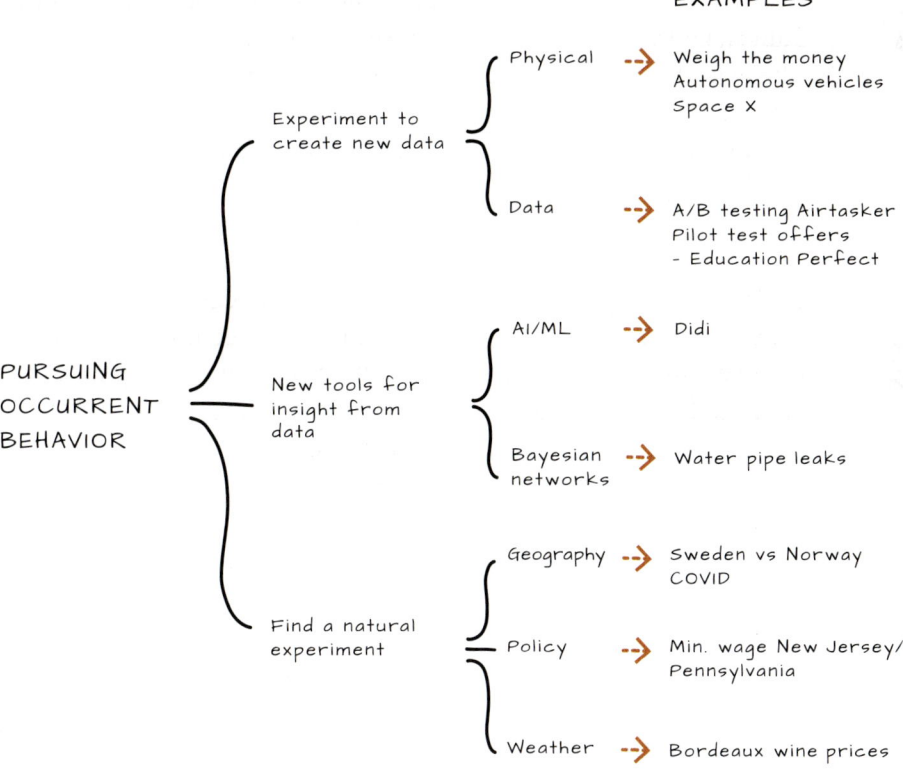

EXAMPLES

Experiment to create new data
- Physical → Weigh the money / Autonomous vehicles / Space X
- Data → A/B testing Airtasker / Pilot test offers / - Education Perfect

PURSUING OCCURRENT BEHAVIOR

New tools for insight from data
- AI/ML → Didi
- Bayesian networks → Water pipe leaks

Find a natural experiment
- Geography → Sweden vs Norway COVID
- Policy → Min. wage New Jersey/ Pennsylvania
- Weather → Bordeaux wine prices

Exhibit 3.2

Experiment to Create New Data

If tomorrow's strategic and operating environment is going to be like today's, there isn't a strong case for experimenting. But if rapid change and high uncertainty are part of an industry's structure and dynamics (what we face in nearly every situation today), then experimenting is imperative to developing the case for action. Yes, experimenting takes time and money, the results are not guaranteed, and the only thing that's certain is that there will be some failures. With trial comes error. But, knowing this, companies can turn trial and error to their advantage: They can try small but impactful experiments, framing the most important questions (each of which should have a hypothesis), and they should fail fast, and try, try again. Remember that there are costs to *not* experimenting: Like it or not, someone else is trying to disrupt the industry, and perhaps is trying to disrupt your company in particular.

Autonomous Vehicle Experiments

The old adage that everyone loves a winner isn't true when it comes to autonomous vehicles (AVs). If anything, people love to read about AV failures. Some accounts are humorous, like the AV in San Francisco that took off and reparked when a policeman approached! Others are grim: In 2016, the sensor of a Tesla Model S sedan failed to distinguish between a large white 18-wheel tractor trailer crossing the highway and the sky, killing the Tesla owner. Crashes demonstrate the need for additional rigorous experimentation to meet safety requirements. But so far reports of AV accidents show that only two out of 187 collisions were linked to systems performance; the rest were caused by human error.[4]

AVs are still in the early stage of a safety journey not dissimilar to the one taken by cars in the early twentieth century. But like so much else, things are moving more rapidly now. One hundred years ago there were 18.65 automobile-related deaths for every 100 million miles. Tesla estimates that there is one fatality for every 320 million miles covered by self-driving cars in autopilot mode—a massive improvement since the days of the Model T. At today's leading autonomous vehicle automakers, the learning rate is steep, with AI learning on a dataset of the safest 10,000 drivers. Continuous experiments are the fastest way to reach peak safety performance.

Yet formidable challenges persist. For example, sensors can be no less reliable when faced with heavy traffic, stormy skies, or road signs defaced with graffiti; they must work in all weather conditions and population densities. They must also navigate roundabouts, which are common in the UK and other countries. Like human drivers, AVs don't always get roundabouts right—at least not yet.

The likes of Waymo, Alibaba's AutoX, Baidu, and Cruise are developing machine learning algorithms that capture the properties of the surrounding environment and predict possible changes to those surroundings. These tasks are mainly divided into four subtasks: regression algorithms, cluster algorithms, decision matrix algorithms, and pattern recognition. But as yet there is no standardized metric that ensures that the machine learning algorithms used in AVs are safe. Self-driving cars need to learn and adapt to different situations so they can detect and interpret objects they come across.

At the same time, the only sure way "the road"—that is, drivers, cyclists, pedestrians, and, ultimately, the regulators who answer to them—can learn to understand and adapt to AVs is to see and experience AVs in daily driving. Building trust between the public and AVs will be fundamental to their mass adoption. To achieve what the automotive world calls "Level 5" (complete hands-off-the-wheel driving, or cars that are completely driver-free), it will be necessary to rationalize the governing rules. There are currently no regulations sufficient for a whole autonomous driving system in any country. Even in the "simple" case of Australia, more than 50 federal and state laws would need to be amended—amounting to nothing less than a complete overhaul of the country's motoring insurance system and traffic network. That will only happen when AVs become the accepted norm.

Space X: Relentless Experimenting

Time flies for Space X: It's now 20 years into its mission to revolutionize space exploration. Elon Musk's vision and drive for the company are the stuff of legend. What is less well understood is the company's modus operandi: To substantially lower the cost of space exploration, it experiments relentlessly. Musk understood right from the start that the price to launch had to be as low as possible. Moving down the cost curve required increased frequency of launches.[5]

Space X engineers learned quickly to make small moves that add up to big improvements by repeatedly testing new hypotheses. This rapid test-and-improve approach enables them to acquire new information at a reasonable cost, and to scale up their body of knowledge.[6] They refer to their decision system as "fly, test, fail, fix." One unique challenge Space X set out to solve was how to make its space rocket components reusable. Historically, the large first-stage boosters and the nose cone have accounted for 60% of a rocket's total cost.[7] Engineers saved 10% by recovering the rocket's nose cone in nets. Space X pioneered the use of 3D-printed metal parts in rocket engines and PICA-X composite heat shielding, which NASA had invented but never used. Space X also shifted away from a cost-plus fee model to making roughly 80% of the components in-house. That helped lower the cost per launch significantly.

Space X also benefited from the frequency of its launches by being able to carry out experiments in space. During the 30-year period of its space shuttle program, NASA averaged 4.5 flights per year. Space X averaged 5.3 flights per year from 2002 to 2021, close to 20% more. The tempo picked up in 2021 when Space X launched a record 31 rockets in orbit, up from 26 the prior year. In early 2022 it was launching three to five missions per month.

More frequent launches dramatically reduce the cost of putting a kilogram of mass into space. For the period from the 1970s to the early 2000s, this cost was largely unchanged. It cost NASA $1.5 billion to haul 27,500 kilograms into space, a cost of $54,550 per kilogram.[8] Space X slashed the per-kilogram cost down to $2,720, a reduction of 95% (see Exhibit 3.3).[9]

A/B Testing at Airtasker

Airtasker is a marketplace for local services, number-one of its kind in Australia for what we loosely call "household chores." Founded by CEO Tim Fung in 2012 and now serving over one million customers, it works like this: You post the task you need someone to perform, say cleaning out the shed or being a waiter at a special function, set the budget you're prepared to pay, and pick the best quote you receive online. Airtasker's initial business model

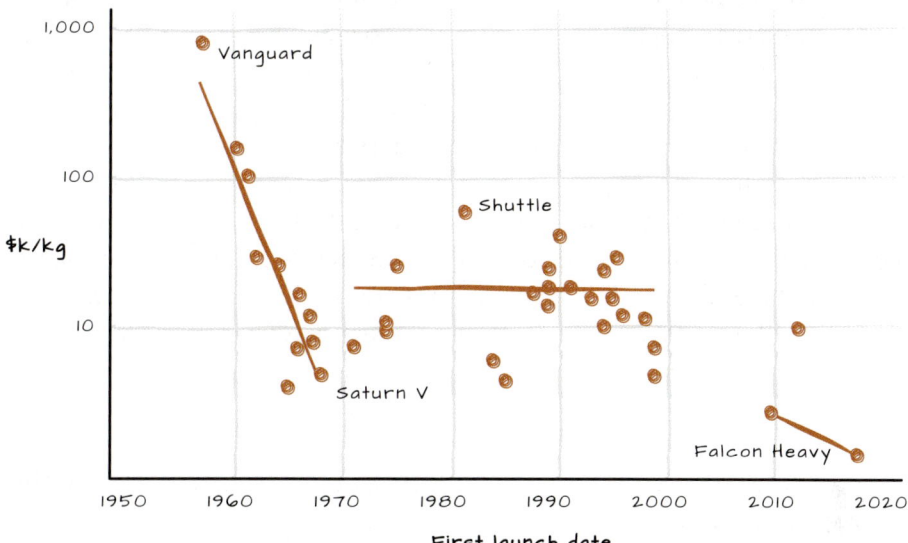

LAUNCH COST PER KILOGRAM TO LOW EARTH ORBIT VS. FIRST LAUNCH DATE

Exhibit 3.3

SOURCE: H. JONES, NASA, CONFERENCE PAPER, 48TH INTERNATIONAL CONFERENCE ON ENVIRONMENTAL SYSTEMS 2018.

was simple. Posting the task is free, but the provider on average receives 87 cents on a dollar and the platform 13 cents. While free posting naturally encourages widespread use of the marketplace, Fung started to question whether Airtasker could refine its pricing policy. In particular, he wanted to know what might be the impact on the business of imposing a charge on the customer for accepting the provider's bid (a bit like a booking fee).

Airtasker decided to run an A/B test, what Fung calls the A, B, C, D, E trial, to see how customers would respond in practice. Using the Optimizely A/B testing software, the team experimented over a week with a sample of 10,000 jobs by setting booking fees variously at zero, 1%, 3%, 6%, and 10%. The result? Nothing changed! There was no price sensitivity over this fee range. Indeed, when Fung added a 10% booking fee to Airtasker's pricing, revenue increased by 50%.

But the story does not end there. Six months later the company reran the A/B test with a higher booking fee and found this time that demand dropped off a cliff. It seems that there was what economists call a "kinked" demand curve, inelastic over a wide range of fees then highly elastic at the point where fees are deemed too high by customers.

Creating data through A/B testing is now almost second nature to Fung. He distrusts theory, preferring to attach weight to what customers reveal through their behavior in the tests, not what they say or what he thinks they might do. Digital natives like him believe in testing and share the statistician's belief that "it's all in the data."

Education Perfect: What the Educators Learned

The emerging sector of educational technology, or EdTech—the hardware and software of learning and education—includes massive online open courses (MOOCs) and interactive teaching tools (such as connected whiteboards). Early-stage companies in EdTech have global aspirations, but they face significant barriers, not least of which are the significant costs of acquiring customers and winning acceptance in school districts worldwide. Understandably, it's hard to create practicable data in the face of so much uncertainty and variation.

Consider the New Zealand–based EdTech company, Education Perfect. In late January 2020, during Chinese New Year, the COVID-19 pandemic was beginning to disrupt and then close schools. The pandemic soon accelerated, affecting countries all over the world. Teachers had only days (and sometimes mere hours) to introduce remote learning. Education Perfect CEO Alex Burke understood that he had to respond quickly. "We made a decision to offer a free trial over the period closing out on May 1st," Burke told us. "Over eight weeks we had an additional 500,000 students trialing the platform, and the number of countries accessing it jumped from 18 to 60."[10]

Education Perfect turned the trial offer into an inflection point. First, it saw a 65% renewal rate from the trial, adding 5% to revenue growth and creating value for years to come. The experiment certainly paid off in terms of lifetime value (LTV) to customer acquisition cost (CAC) (see Exhibit 3.4). But beyond the immediate boost to revenue, the trial provided data on other schools that said they would like to be contacted in the future when Education Perfect's systems had improved. The company generated valuable customer experience data, and this new knowledge will help ground expectations as it scales up.

EDUCATION PERFECT COVID-19 EXPERIMENT
- 8WEEK FREE TRIAL JANUARY 2020

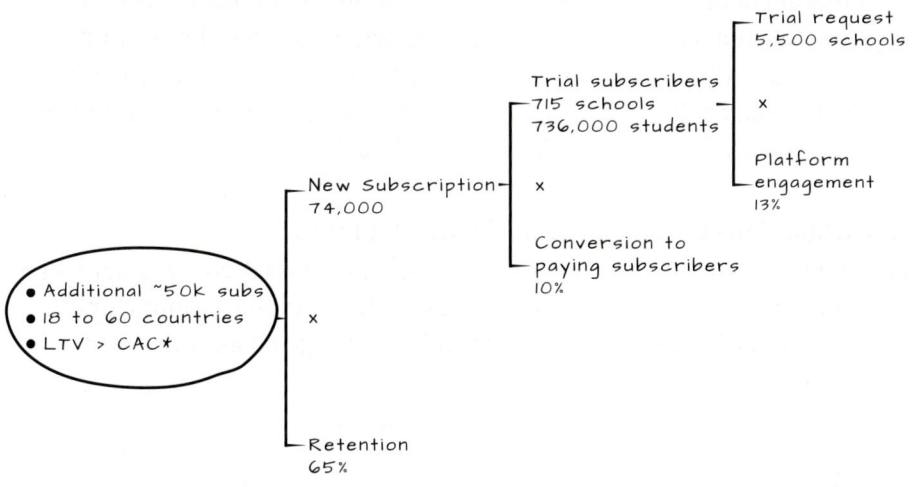

* LTV = Long Term Value; CAC = Customer Acquisition Cost

Exhibit 3.4
SOURCE: EDUCATION PERFECT.

Other tech companies with which we are familiar have a full suite of experiments underway, from R&D trials of product, to design tests of features, to trials of online sales versus instore sales, and to in-house versus user-supported customer experience. They experiment relentlessly because the payoff from winning is so high—both in getting to market with the right product or service features, and getting there ahead of competitors.

New Tools and Approaches

Experimentation is not cost free. It's always worth conducting a cost-benefit analysis, and to be realistic about what *cost* and *benefit* mean. Cost needs to be measured not just in currency but also in time. Could organizational attention be unduly consumed by minor, incremental experiments, particularly ones that take ages to perform and analyze? On the other hand, what is the benefit, not just in terms of what the competitive landscape looks like now, but as it may be transformed if a hypothesis proves right? Experiments should always yield data—even if the data point is simply "this doesn't work" or "we can't draw a conclusion from these results." But the decision whether or not to perform experiments will be easier to make if the costs of experiments are lessened, particularly by using new tools and approaches.

Jean Liu Tries Things Differently at Didi

Didi is a ride-hailing service from China. It is similar to Uber; it operates private vehicles, taxis, bicycles, buses, and carpooling services. In fact, it is more than three times bigger than Uber as measured by drivers and users.[11] Didi has 380 million users across 400 cities worldwide. Didi's willingness to embrace occurrent behavior and experiment with machine learning enabled it to defeat Uber in China. In the process, Didi gave rise to China's first female tech baron: Jean Liu.

When Liu first arrived in Beijing as a Goldman Sachs executive from Hong Kong, she was baffled by the severity of congestion in the Chinese capital and by the rationing of vehicle licenses. Even Liu, for whom money was not a significant constraint, was unable to buy a car: One simply could not have a car without a license. So she was forced to rely on taxis, often enduring "long waits in the rain, or worse being ignored by passing drivers."[12] These same frustrations, she soon realized, must be equally common for millions of other people living under conditions of rising demand and limited resources.[13] The frustration of hailing a taxi prodded Liu to pursue a position with Didi, a Chinese start-up that was already challenging China's inefficient taxi dispatching system. Didi initially rebuffed her, but she refused to take no for an answer. She lobbied founder Cheng Wei until he relented, and offered her the position of COO.[14]

When Liu began, Didi was facilitating 600,000 daily trips. Liu grew that to 25 million rides per day. She set out to find a model that best accommodated the 800 million urban Chinese who need greater access to mobility. Liu appreciated that the only way to understand and get fully immersed in Didi's services was to interact with its passengers. So, she would find time in her schedule to travel around Beijing as a Didi driver for the sole purpose of interacting with ordinary Didi users to learn and improve the company—microscale experimentation.

Liu invited Didi's drivers to send feedback to her personally over Weibo—no easy feat, when there are 13 million drivers! The experience heightened her appreciation of the importance of feedback; it inspired her to improve passenger and driver satisfaction.[15] And it also allowed her to identify a blind spot. "We were too focused on technology," Liu realized, "we believed technology could solve everything."[16] As a result, she began to move Didi away from an Uber-like exclusively online-only business model. For example, unlike Uber, which only trains new drivers online, Didi developed a program for 2000 "driver buddies" to personally train new drivers, thereby ensuring that feedback would be effectively communicated to the new recruits. Through engaging on the platform and speaking with paying customers, Liu made it her mission to incorporate feedback into the organization's working model.[17]

Some changes worked and some didn't. But relentless experimenting led Liu to the conclusion that Didi was not fundamentally a technology business at all. It was a people business. She saw how important it was, for example, for Didi to respond to assaults that had taken place in its vehicles; it needed to build trust with consumers. So it began to publish a monthly risk report, becoming the first ride-hailing company to publish monthly data on disputes, accidents, and even criminal cases.[18] The benefits of experimenting are so great that Liu now insists that her senior executives drive and pick up passengers themselves.[19] This helps those executives better understand the mindsets of Didi's millions of drivers and hundreds of millions of active users.[20]

Today, innovative changes allow the company to blend high- and low-tech solutions, combining machine learning with millions of relatively low-skilled drivers. Liu has added more than 13,000 new corporate employees to Didi, half of them data scientists and engineers pursuing AI solutions. The result has been some remarkable breakthroughs. By tapping driver feedback, Didi has used real-time car data to optimize traffic lights in the eastern city of Jinan. Didi algorithms now power smart traffic lights, cutting congestion by 10%. Didi also uses an AI-powered arbitration system, which helps judge whether a driver or passenger is at fault should a ride be canceled, which has cut complaints by one-third.[21] And, through AI and the study of weather forecasts of cities, the company is now in a position to quickly increase vehicle availability in areas about to be deluged by rain. Didi, in other words, knows when customers may need to hail a car before customers realize it themselves.

The Hidden 80:20 Rule: Predicting Underground Water Pipe Failure

We've heard a lot in recent years about "big data" and the sophistication of data analysis techniques. But what if there is only *sparse* data about a problem, and the problem solvers only have conventional tools such as multiple regression, which are of low predictive value? Dr. Fang Chen, a PhD in AI and a distinguished professor, faced precisely this problem when the water authority in her home town of Sydney asked her: "How do we predict critical water pipe failures in advance?"

Sydney has thousands of kilometers of critical water main (CWM) pipes, mostly underground. The pipes are widely taken for granted—until they break. And when they do, the social and financial costs of failure are huge, ranging from flooding to traffic disruption. While preventive maintenance of CWMs is approximately 10 times cheaper than reactive repairs, it is difficult to assess pipes that are underground. Utility managers can typically assess only 1% of the network length each year. Therefore, their data analysts have long tried to predict where pipe failures are most likely to occur, so that they can focus their preventive maintenance efforts there and minimize repair costs.

Imagine that you were asked to solve this problem. Perhaps your initial hypothesis would be that the *oldest* pipes would be most likely to fail. It stands to reason, after all, that the principle of "first in, first out" would apply. Early research in the 1980s used such time-dependent models, which explicitly assumed that older pipes are more likely to break than newly laid ones. But that hypothesis didn't hold and therefore didn't provide the solution. Since then there have been experiments with multiple different statistical models and machine learning approaches and it turns out that there are many reasons why pipes break. These can be classified into multiple categories, primarily: (1) the condition and age of the pipe, (2) the type of environment in which the pipe is laid (e.g., the corrosivity of the soil), (3) the pipe manufacturer's quality, and (4) service conditions (e.g., water pressure).[22]

Most CWM pipes can have a lifespan of more than 100 years, during which they rarely if ever break, while the collection of robust data on pipe failures is mostly too recent to aid prediction. In the case of Dr. Chen's team, about 99% of the pipes they considered did not fail or failed only once over a 12-year observation period. Their overall pipe failure data was therefore incredibly sparse.

To learn more, Dr. Chen's team invented a new type of nonparametric Bayesian machine learning model that performed well even with sparse data. She and her colleagues estimated the probability of water pipe failure based on multiple attributes. Not only was her model able to predict more than 80% of water pipe failures before they occurred within the top 20% pipe risk rankings shown in Exhibit 3.5—significantly more than other failure prediction tools—its flexibility meant that it could be used for other problems that have sparse data, such as predicting where cracks will occur on the Sydney Harbour Bridge (cracks on the Harbour Bridge are also extremely rare).

Almost all other existing state-of-the-art prediction tools relied on parametric models; it was the nonparametric property of Dr. Chen's model that made it more successful. Parametric models make assumptions about the attributes of the pipe. For example, they assume that cast-iron pipes are more likely to break than PVC pipes. But nonparametric models make no such assumptions. This allows for more flexible solutions. The nonparametric property of the team's model allowed them to discover, for example, that pipes in a regional area were

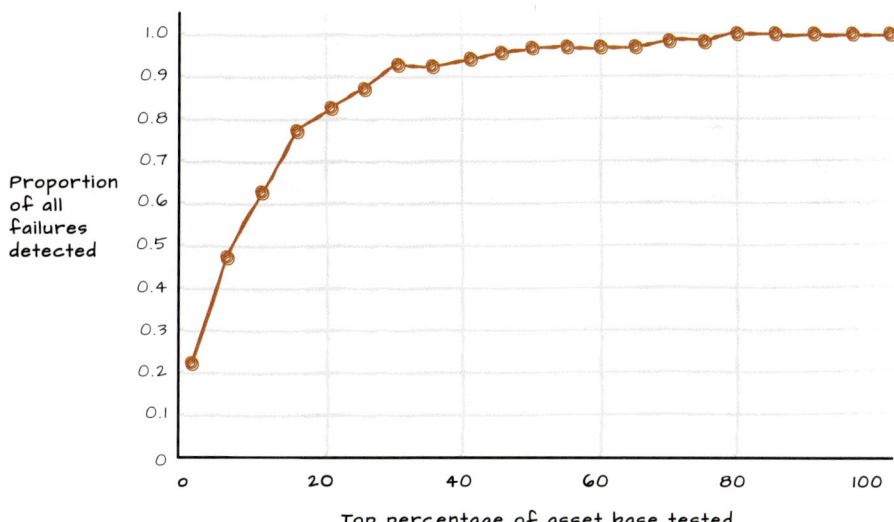

WATER PIPE PREDICTION PERFORMANCE (ALL PIPES)

Proportion of all failures detected

Top percentage of asset base tested

Exhibit 3.5

SOURCE: PROFESSOR FANG CHEN.

failing more often than pipes in Sydney, even though the pipe and soil attributes were very similar. After isolating many attributes, Dr. Chen's team noticed that the regional area of Wollongong was more newly formed and more unstable than Sydney. This geological difference, therefore, may have caused the increased pipe failures.

During 2020, Dr. Chen's team collaborated with 13 water utility, university, and industry partners coordinated by the NSW Smart Sensing Network to further improve their nonparametric model with more and better-quality data, as well as a new attribute, MNF (minimum nightly flow).[23] Their results show that by inspecting 20% of pipes, they can detect about 80% of pipe failures and predict within 200 meters where those pipe failures will occur. Thanks to this work, the annual industry inspection standard of Sydney Water has increased from just 1% of pipes to 2.5% of pipes; that means that over eight years, companies should be able to predict 80% of pipe failures—a remarkable improvement.

Water utility partners in Australia and the UK are currently testing Dr. Chen's model, which continues to benefit from new field data and to improve its water pipe failure prediction rate. Already, the solutions have saved 5,000 megaliters of water (the size of 2,000 Olympic-sized swimming pools) and more than $10 million in water. That's a testament to a mindset that is open to experimentation and novel analytical approaches—even when the uncertainty is high and the data points are sparse.

Find a Natural Experiment

A natural experiment exists when two otherwise similar decision makers pursue different policies and achieve different results. Natural experiments allow us to compare problem solving strategies under uncertainty in situations where a randomized control trial or A/B test would be unethical. The classic cases are twin cities that have similar populations but different policies.

Sweden versus Norway Responding to COVID

The responses to the COVID-19 outbreak in March 2020 provide a rich set of public health problem solving comparisons. One of the most striking is of two Scandinavian countries, Sweden and Norway, which share a long border and have similar populations on nearly every demographic dimension.

Both are modern social democracies with a strong welfare state and high-quality universal public healthcare. Both had minority coalition governments at the time. Both have well-regarded public health planning: The Global Health Security Index ranked Sweden at 7 and Norway at 16 for preparedness for handling an infectious disease outbreak the year before the pandemic.[24]

As is now well known, Sweden was one of the countries that took the most hands-off approach to managing the public health crisis, while Norway's was much stricter. Both countries coordinate public health strongly at the national level, but whereas Norway's agencies tend to be directly controlled by government ministries, Sweden's agencies are more autonomous. What played out was a nationally coordinated and strongly precautionary set of policies in Norway, and an approach strongly controlled by a single agency in Sweden, the Agency for Public Health, and particularly by state epidemiologist Dr. Anders Tegnell. The prime minister and other relevant government ministers in Sweden played a much more passive role in managing the crisis.

While never publicly confirmed, it is thought that early in the pandemic, at a time when death rates were not well understood and before vaccines were developed, Tegnell was following a herd immunity strategy rather than a precautionary approach, as was the case in Norway. He argued against most restrictions on gatherings, including in schools and restaurants, and against the use of masks indoors.

We can see the differences in this policy comparison in 2020, early in the pandemic, in Exhibit 3.6.[25]

Substantial differences in problem solving around what was an unanticipated epidemic led to large differences in health outcomes. In Norway the excess death rate of 7.2 per 100,000 over the 2020–2021 period was relatively low. Sweden's excess death rate in the same period was nearly 13 times higher than that of its neighbor (see Exhibit 3.7).[26] That said, Sweden's excess death rate of 91.2 over the first two pandemic years was lower than the 140 average across Western Europe, where a broader range of demographic and policy solutions interacted.

Some in Sweden and in other countries with regimes that were less restrictive have argued that pandemic problem solving involves a necessary trade-off between loss of life and restrictions on movement that affect the national economy. Norway, as it happens, had significantly better economic results than Sweden during the first year of the

EARLY PANDEMIC POLICY RESPONSE

	Norway		Sweden
• 31 Jan:	Directorate of Health temporarily authorized to make binding decisions		
• 6 Mar:	Visits to elder care suspended		
• 11 Mar:	Lockdown (no assemblies over 500, schools, restaurants and most events suspended; mandatory quarantine for visitors)	• 12 Mar:	No assemblies of >500
• 16 Mar:	Border closed	• 17 Mar:	Distance learning for some schools
• 25 Mar:	No assemblies of 5 or more	• 27 Mar:	No assemblies over 50; visits to eldercare suspended
• 24 Apr:	Testing capacity of 5 per week in municipalities mandated	• 16 Apr:	Communicable Disease Act expands government powers
• 17 Jun:	Mask mandate enacted	• 4 Nov:	Some limitations on number of people in restaurants and bars
		•	No mask mandate

Exhibit 3.6

pandemic, although because of Norway's status as a major oil producer the two countries are not a perfect natural experiment in economic terms.[27]

Countries weigh many factors when preparing for unexpected events, and when thinking about how their plans might play out. The natural experiment in Scandinavia has given us useful new data for countries updating their public health preparations in a post-pandemic world.

Insights into Employment and the Minimum Wage

For decades, economists taught us that wages were set by the marginal productivity of labor. At the tails of distributions, this is certainly true. If the minimum wage were $1,000,000 per hour, for example, we can be confident that unemployment would increase. Large fast-food restaurants

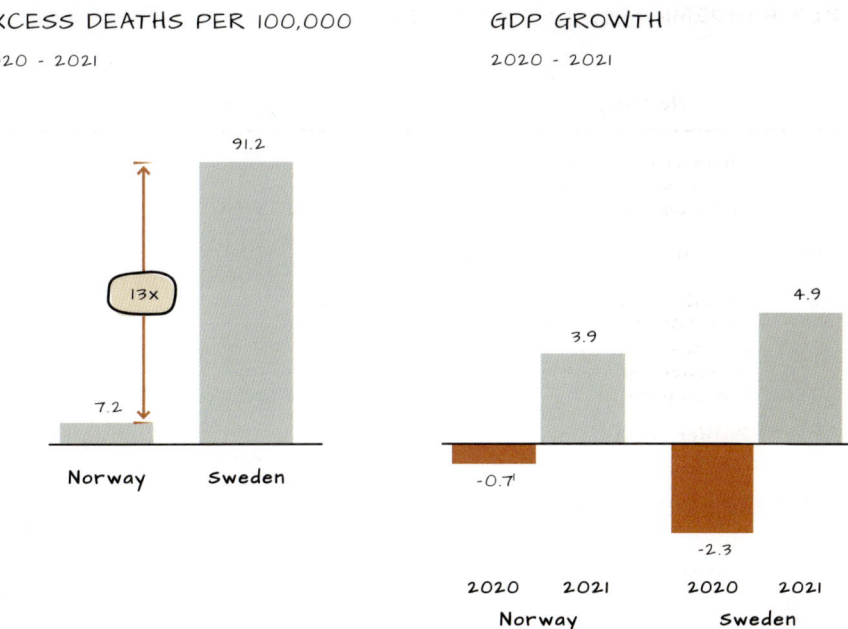

EXCESS DEATHS PER 100,000

2020 - 2021

GDP GROWTH

2020 - 2021

Exhibit 3.7

SOURCES: *THE LANCET*; THE ORGANISATION FOR ECONOMIC CO-OPERATION AND DEVELOPMENT.

in the United States are responding to rising minimum wages by shifting to greater automation.[28] But what do the data say about harder, in-between cases? Economists David Card and Alan Krueger set out to find the answer, examining the impact of raising New Jersey's minimum wage in April 1992 from $4.25 to $5.05 per hour, and surveying 410 fast-food restaurants in New Jersey and eastern Pennsylvania before and after the increase.[29] The ingenious nature of this natural experiment lay in utilizing a control group of fast-food stores in eastern Pennsylvania where there was no increase in the minimum wage. The economists collected data in two waves—a first wave prior to the minimum wage change and a second wave some six months after the New Jersey increase.

Card and Krueger found that even with the wage increase, full-time employment rose in New Jersey relative to that in Pennsylvania. The economists tested for demand shocks in New Jersey that might explain the finding, and tested whether the mix of full- and part-time workers might have changed, as a minimum wage increase could have led to the substitution of full-time higher-wage workers and capital. There was no clear evidence for these factors. They checked to see if there had been a reduction in fringe benefits, finding no indication that there had been. They explored the possibility that employers had cut back on free or reduced-price meals to offset the minimum wage increase (they didn't). Card and Krueger did find, though, that the wage increases were passed on through higher price increases in New Jersey than in Pennsylvania.

David Card received the Nobel Prize for Economics in 2021 for his empirical contributions to labor economics. His work has emphasized how twin cities, neighboring states, or geographic units that make a policy change different from an adjoining area provide fertile ground to run a natural experiment and help solve important social problems like establishing the minimum wage level.

What Makes for a Great Bordeaux Wine?

Each March some 6,000 visitors arrive in Bordeaux for *en primeur* week. Here, while the wines are still in barrels, contracts are set for their price in two years' time. Setting futures prices is believed to date back to 58 AD, when grapes were bought on the vine. Today, Bordeaux wine is big business: More than 200 labels produce an aggregate of over 500 million bottles each year, at auction prices that can reach over $500 per bottle. Wine futures markets play an important role in pricing. In theory they provide discounts for buyers, ensure availability of supply, and offer risk takers a healthy financial reward based on wine price appreciation. To achieve attractive returns, the *en primeur* price must be a good predictor that the wine will mature into a highly valued vintage. But is it?

Enter a famous Princeton University economist who happens to love wine, Orley Ashenfelter.[30] He set out to answer the question of whether prices set at vintage are good indicators of long-term value. His answer was a sober No! Ashenfelter discovered that the *en primeur* system acted more like an agriculture income stabilization system than an especially informed indicator of long-term value. *En primeur* purchasing, he found, generated a 3% real rate of return for investors. This is effectively a return for tying up capital, similar to futures pricing in commodities.

Ashenfelter's conclusions ran counter to the conventional wisdom of experts, and of tradition. His reasoning was superb: He chose to focus on how the weather influences wine quality and price, because "the case of weather in Bordeaux presents a very nice natural experiment." As he explained: "The weather differs sufficiently from year to year and the quality of the grapes is recorded sufficiently (through wine prices) to measure weather's true effects on quality. A lot is known about weather effects on quality from past vintages." In general, Ashenfelter said, "high-quality vintages for Bordeaux wines correspond to the years in which August and September are dry, the growing season is warm, and the previous winter has been wet."[31] This observation allowed him to set about measuring the effects with different variables, and collect clearer data.

Ashenfelter was able to explain a whopping 83% of the variation in the average prices of Bordeaux vintages with this approach. As a practiced economist, he developed a multiple regression model of the prices of wine based on several variables. The age of the vintage was one; it explained about 20% of the variance. But weather factors were the main drivers: The average temperature over the growing season (April–September), the presence of rain in August (a negative), rain in the months preceding the vintage, and average temperatures in September were all important. Later he fermented the results down to an equation:

$$\text{Wine quality} = 12.145 / .00117^{*} \text{ Winter rainfall} + .0614 \text{ Average growing season temp} - 0.00386 \text{ Harvest rainfall}$$

Forbes reported that wine guru Robert Parker was unimpressed—he remarked, "I'd hate to be invited to his house to drink wine." However, those who followed Ashenfelter's advice made a lot of money by betting "against the house."[32] Interestingly, Ashenfelter's data was not proprietary to any one producer, being widely available to a wide array of producers and investors alike. The solution did not require an *en primeur* week trip to Bordeaux, however much fun that would be—just a brilliant natural experiment.

Can You Experiment Too Much?

About 700 BC, the Greek poet Hesiod famously counseled for moderation in all things. Many centuries later the Irish playwright Oscar Wilde parried that "moderation is a fatal thing." "Nothing succeeds," he quipped, "like excess." Give Hesiod his due: It *is* possible to experiment too much. The choice to experiment or not to experiment comes down to costs and benefits. When everything has to be trialed, it may be just another form of risk aversion. Experimenting too much can lead to what is quaintly called "pilot purgatory": a place where pilot tests abound but initiatives to scale up the results never seem to happen. A survey of Internet of things (IoT) applications showed that "84 percent of companies were stuck in pilot mode for over a year and 28 percent for over two years."[33]

Scaling solutions is critical for start-ups and new businesses. It requires problem solving skill to identify false positives and avoid sweeping conclusions from trial results, and to recognize the indirect effects from a trial called spillovers that dilute advantage. As economist John List pointed out, "scaling in the end is a weakest link problem."[34] Great problem solvers are rigorous about how they design experiments: They know what they are trying to test, how that fits with the direction they want to go, and how to correct course rapidly as they move ahead. They find the critical path, doing experiments in the order that knocks out weak contenders fastest.

Having a mantra like Space X's *fly, test, fail, fix* helps overcome the risk of pilot purgatory; it brings the perspectives of high consequence and value of information to the experiment. If the information isn't particularly valuable—if you know enough so that the cost of standing still is already greater than the cost of knowing more—then go forward.

That guidance applies well beyond high tech. Would you expect to hear an NGO say they plan to fail fast? Probably not. Yet that was precisely how The Nature Conservancy approached its Pacific tuna program for sustainable catch. The Conservancy required evidence rapidly to support scaling or course-correcting its program, so it embarked on testing multiple hypotheses through experimentation. Failing fast fitted perfectly.

Bringing Occurrent Behavior into Your Own Organization

To our knowledge, occurrent behavior is not defined in strategy and organization textbooks. But like the mindset itself, we know it when we see it. How far your organization should head down the occurrent behavior path depends on a few factors. Here are the most important:

1. *Assess your need for relentless experimenting.* Do you have high-consequence choices to make? Do you face consequential uncertainty, or are you confident that you have enough information to move forward? Try to put yourself on a 5-point scale from No Need to High Need for relentless experimenting.

2. *Measure your measuring.* How much experimenting are you currently doing to reduce uncertainty? Zero? Some experimenting, but patchy? Relentlessly experimenting? Can you identify the experiments you are conducting?

3. *Invest in digital and analytics capabilities.* Everything from data collection and governance to machine learning can yield cutting-edge proprietary insight. Are you at parity, leading, or lagging in data analytics capability compared to industry leaders? Do you have platforms on which to undertake experiments and analyze results?

4. *Be like Bayes.* Is your problem solving based on hypotheses? How do you marshal evidence? If you are conducting experiments, what hypotheses are you seeking to test? Are these clearly set out before and during the experiment? Do you discuss prior probabilities and how they are derived? Do you update probabilities based on new evidence?

5. *Articulate why you aren't experimenting.* What is standing in the way of more experimenting? Do the costs really outweigh the benefits? Are there ways to reduce the cost, or obstacles that you can remove? For example, can a Bayesian adaptive trial be used rather than an expensive randomized control trial? Is the problem inadequate resources? Or is the problem a culture of instant answers? Or fear of failure?

6. *Parse the process.* Do you need to review key processes like design, product development, and marketing in order to let occurrent behavior flourish? Are they too "grooved" to provide quick answers and economy of effort? Do any processes need a complete overhaul to bring in more experimentation?

7. *Think in outcomes.* Can you define what a successful shift to occurrent behavior will look like in 12–18 months? Will the conversations about tackling uncertainty start to sound Bayesian in the sense that you know the most informative experiments to conduct? Will your rate of experimentation have noticeably increased? Will we expect major insight to come from creating new data and novel analysis?

Chapter 4
Collective Intelligence

A Clockmaker, a Prize, and a King

On the evening of October 22, 1707, 2,000 British seamen lost their lives when four warships ran aground on rocks near the Scilly Isles, off the coast of Cornwall. The result of a navigational error, this widely publicized human tragedy significantly raised consciousness in Britain about the "longitude problem," the most urgent and elusive scientific challenge of the day.

Without being able to establish longitude, a geographic coordinate that specifies the east–west position of a point on the surface of the earth, captains of ships had had to rely for centuries on what they called "dead reckoning" (steering by gut instinct). "Every great captain in the Age of Exploration became lost at sea despite the best available charts and compasses," writes Dava Sobel. "From Vasco de Gama to Vasco Nunez de Balboa, from Ferdinand Magellan to Sir Francis Drake—they all got where they were going willy-nilly, by forces attributed to good luck or the grace of God."[1]

All that was to change in July 1714, when Queen Anne gave her royal assent to an Act of Parliament that offered a reward up to £20,000 (a whopping £1.5 million in today's money) to anyone who could solve the longitude puzzle to an accuracy to half a degree, or plus or minus three seconds a day.

The first Longitude Board, which oversaw the prize, included the esteemed Sir Isaac Newton, who stated categorically that he expected a solution to come from what he called the "regular notions of the clock-work universe." Guiding ships at sea, he proclaimed, would be determined by "lunar distance methods." Edmond Halley, of comet fame, with the title of Astronomer Royal, was equally adamant, not to say dogmatic. He observed that the Longitude Board ". . . would not welcome a mechanical answer to what it saw as an astronomical question."[2]

Against this backdrop of an attractive prize and the Board's bias against mechanical solutions, John Harrison, a successful clockmaker, turned his attention to marine timekeeping in 1727. His goal was to create a precise time-keeping device that would be accurate in the raging sea. Knowing accurate time, and knowing accurate speed through other means, the seamen would know just how far they had gone. Harrison put his first proposal for a marine chromometer to the Board in 1731; four years later his H-1 design, weighing a hefty 75 pounds, was trialed successfully by the *Centurion*'s voyage to Lisbon, Portugal. Finally, in 1759, he won the prize with the H-4, a precise device trimmed down to only 5 inches in diameter.

For the next decade Harrison was involved in wrangles, some of them farcical, over the distribution of the prize money. At one point Reverend Nevil Maskelyne, Astronomer Royal, on behalf of the Board, arrived at Harrison's premises with a warrant for the arrest of the sea clocks! But by 1772, following the intervention of King George, Harrison had won the day over the lunar distance advocates and solved the longitude problem with his marine chromometer.

The Longitude Prize remains a remarkable story of how a contest can bring collective intelligence to bear on a great unsolved problem. The subplot is how assumptions about where the solution will come from can hinder innovation, in this case from the physicists and astronomers and their influence on the Longitude Board.

Have Experts Lost Their Luster?

The Longitude Prize episode is also a lesson in why we all need to be alert to the views of outsiders, who are often without conventional expertise. In management consulting, a business we know well, the industry experts we called upon in our early days had typically served numerous clients and had often worked in the sector before entering consulting. They would typically help guide our problem solving so we didn't reinvent the wheel, go down rabbit holes, or overlook important issues. They had a "mud map" of where to look for problems, and a range of solutions that would or wouldn't work based on their experiences in similar settings. They not only helped our teams be productive but gave clients peace of mind that we weren't making it up as we went along. As we reflect on the experts we worked with two decades ago, however, they were typically in mature industries like steel, oil and gas, and banking that were undergoing only modest rates of change.

The problem today is that even these mature industries are evolving faster than at any other time in our lifetimes. The players, technologies, and rules of competition are no longer fixed. For instance, the steel industry faces a huge challenge to decarbonize carbon steel to make "green steel," with implications for competitiveness that have only been sketchily worked out. The oil and gas industry is grappling with new technology (for example, fracking and deep water production), and facing growing pressure to lessen its impact on the climate. Decentralized finance (DeFi) is transforming banks through blockchain and smart contracts, with tech companies like Apple, Google, and Amazon expanding their role in payments. Is the banking expert still the person who knows regulation and capital requirements, or is it the technologist who understands how to create an app for a digital wallet?

Companies in almost every industry now face the choice either to disrupt themselves, or to be disrupted by new entrants. If the former, they need to go beyond traditional expertise, because the innovation that drives today's disruption invariably involves novel technology, new customer engagement patterns, and revised business models. It often requires an entirely different conception of the boundaries of the market itself, and new ways of conceiving and meeting consumer needs. That puts a premium on having a diverse number of lenses or perspectives—the danger of relying on static expertise is that you end up looking backwards, solving the last problem, not the next one.

Consider the track record of experts in forecasting. Philip Tetlock's work has demonstrated how amateurs routinely outperform domain experts from the world's best thinktanks. These talented forecasters, whom we first met in the Dragonfly Eye mindset, tend to be people who have a reasonable IQ (in the top 20% but not the top 1%), are open minded and intellectually curious, drawn to variety, numerate and probabilistic thinkers, and are flexible enough to alter their view as the facts change.[3]

If amateurs often have an edge over professionals, it is also the case that technology can outdo the domain experts. In medicine, for example, there is growing evidence that a kind of collective intelligence employing artificial intelligence (AI) can provide a more accurate diagnosis than the expert physicians in whom we have traditionally placed our trust. An example is the diagnosis of melanoma, a particularly aggressive form of skin cancer that, if detected early, can be cured in up to 95% of cases. In a recent study, characterized by 17,302 images of melanoma and nevus, far and away the largest-ever dataset of its kind, AI outperformed all 157 dermatologists from 12 university hospitals in Germany.[4] Similarly, analysis of echocardiogram test data shows that AI is 50% better than cardiologists at predicting future cardiac problems.

Diversity of expertise can also help solve complex social problems. In the Dragonfly Eye chapter, we saw how conventional wisdom views child obesity as a health issue linked to nutrition, diet, caloric availability at school, and physical exercise (all which, of course, is at least partly true). But a diverse cross-disciplinary team in Australia, which included an evolutionary biologist, a pediatrician with child obesity expertise, and a Bayesian statistician with machine learning skills, has shown that maternal education is actually the most important causal variable in whether or not a child is obese up to the age of eight.

How do you decide when to use experts and when to put together a diverse team and crowdsourced input? The answer, backed up by research, seems to depend mostly on the level of uncertainty.[5] When problems display high uncertainty and deep complexity, it's time to look beyond experts to collective intelligence, defined as the ability of a group to find more or better solutions than would be found by its members working individually.

Joy's Law

Bill Joy is well known as the co-founder of Sun Microsystems, now part of Oracle. He coined what has become known as Joy's law: "No matter who you are, most of the smart people work for someone else."[6] The logical corollary of Joy's law is that you have to find a way of accessing that intelligence. As Bill Joy put it, "It's better to create an ecology that gets all the world's smartest people toiling in your garden for your own goals. If you rely on your own employees, you'll never solve all your customer's needs."

For some it comes as a shock to have to see the world this way. We've spent a lot of our careers trying to get the smartest people in the room, and linking ourselves to other experts outside the room. The implications for how organizations solve problems are huge. How does our recruiting need to change if we are drawing more on others in the ecosystem? Do we know how to put together really diverse teams? What role should so-called experts play when innovation demands new competence? How do we organize to put Joy's law, and, more broadly, collective intelligence, to work? A simple way to get Joy's Law to work for you is to map the ecosystem of which you're part and decide who you need toiling for you (see Exhibit 4.1).

ECOSYSTEM FOR COLLECTIVE INTELLIGENCE

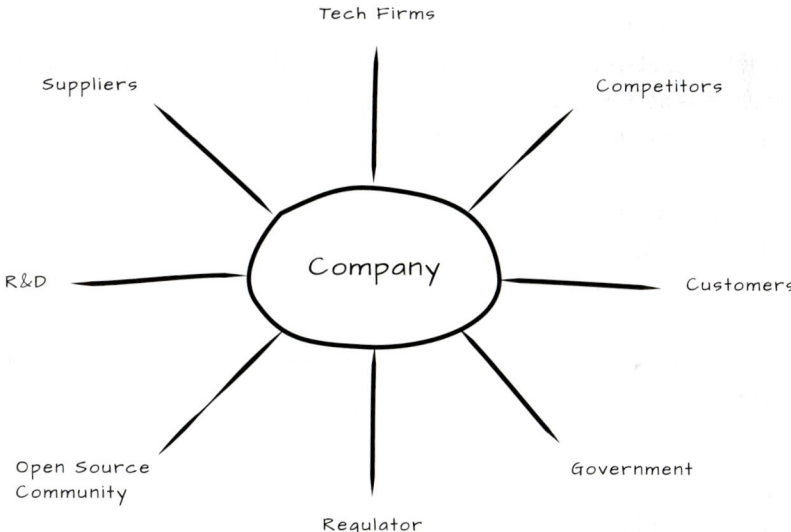

Exhibit 4.1

We asked Vinay Samuel, the founder of software business Zetaris, how it came to be competing with companies 100 times its size. The answer was simple: Vinay says it built off the collective intelligence of others: "We have open source as our relational data base; Apache Spark open source provides the unified analytics engine; we use the natural language processing (NLP) algorithms that Tesla put on their website; and we add our own query optimizer that we employ on the data. Put that together and we have what technology research company Gartner calls a world-leading analytical data virtualization platform"—all with less than $25 million of funding. Vinay's young company is standing on the shoulders of collaborators well outside its own boundaries. Open source software is a special case of Joy's law and a superb example of collaborative crowdsourcing of expertise.

To meet Bill Joy's objective of an ecosystem that gets others toiling in your garden, however, requires the collective intelligence mindset backed by a portfolio of initiatives. We now explore what that means.

Framing Collective Intelligence

When collective intelligence is mentioned in conversation, there is often much nodding that "yes, we know what that is—the wisdom of crowds is guessing how many beans there are in a jar." We think there is a lot more to it. We see collective intelligence playing a key role in how organizations compete. We believe that we should be respectful of experts, but skeptical of historically derived perspectives in settings where the rules are rapidly changing. You should embrace diversity of perspectives in your own teams, and you should look outside your own four walls for rich sources of self-disruption.

Our schema for how to tap collective intelligence involves three branches (see Exhibit 4.2). The first involves crowdsourced expertise. This comes in two varieties, competitive and collaborative. Competitive crowd-sourcing involves prize competitions; collaborative efforts include open source software and massive collaborative experimentation, such as the huge project to find the Higgs-Boson particle. The second branch is collective wisdom. This has several dimensions, including historical community wisdom. We illustrate ancestral wisdom, a subset of community wisdom, with reference to what is now called "right way fire" management in Northern Australia, developed over thousands of years by the original inhabitants. Our third branch involves the combination of human problem solving and artificial intelligence. Under the right conditions (plentiful data, bounded uncertainty), this can be a powerful form of collective intelligence.

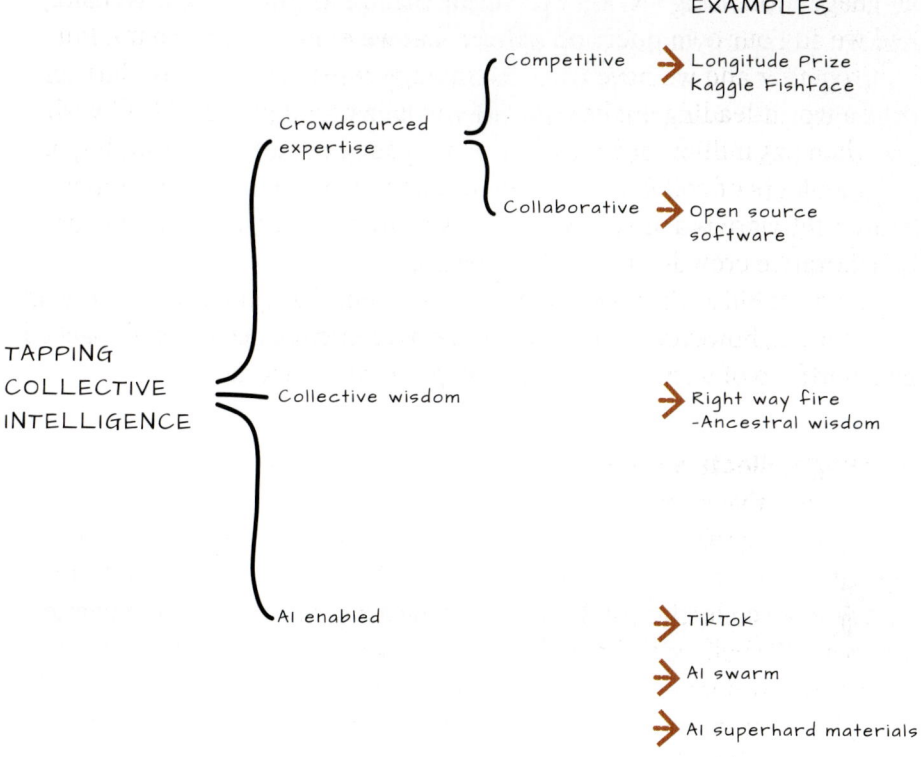

EXAMPLES

Crowdsourced expertise
- Competitive → Longitude Prize / Kaggle Fishface
- Collaborative → Open source software

TAPPING COLLECTIVE INTELLIGENCE

Collective wisdom → Right way fire -Ancestral wisdom

AI enabled → TikTok → AI swarm → AI superhard materials

Exhibit 4.2

Crowdsourced Expertise

Competitive Prizes

Prizes and contests have long helped to spark innovation. The $25,000 Orteig prize for achieving a nonstop flight from New York to Paris was set up in 1919, but five years later it still had not been claimed. The prize was renewed for a further five years and finally won by 25-year-old Charles Lindbergh in 1927. His 3,600-mile, $33\frac{1}{2}$-hour journey in the monoplane *The Spirit of St Louis* revolutionized air transport.

Lindbergh was a charismatic US Mail pilot who had more passion than connections. His efforts to persuade notable aircraft manufacturers to support him foundered in the face of their condition that they would select the pilot—clearly not him. Undaunted, he funded the design and construction of his monoplane with a $15,000 bank loan from two

St. Louis businessmen, a $1,000 contribution from the upstart Ryan Aircraft Company, and $2,000 of his own money.[7]

In 1996, inspired by Lindbergh's story, Peter Diamandis underwrote the modern version of the Orteig prize, which he called the Ansari X prize. Originally aimed at kickstarting the new field of passenger travel to space, its first winners were a team led by legendary aircraft designer Burt Rutan. Today, its ambitions are even greater, with the prize expanded to cover innovation in life sciences, exploration, energy and the environment, and education and development, with individual competitions spanning everything from ocean oil cleanup and gigaton carbon removal to the eradication of poverty.

Kaggle, now owned by Google, is a novel platform also based on the competitive prize concept, aimed at finding innovative solutions through crowdsourcing. Kaggle offers teams datasets with which they can experiment using machine learning algorithms. One contest, which attracted 13,737 entries, challenged participants to predict who survived on the *Titanic*, armed only with access to the ship's manifest of passengers and a list of those saved. The winning algorithms were ones that focused on people without the title Mister, the set that includes women and children! This simple framing worked, as we know that women and children were given priority access to the lifeboats. With access only to the ship's manifest of passengers and survivors, the machine learning algorithms arrived at the right answer.

A number of Kaggle competitions have focused on banking problems, such as loan defaults and creditworthiness, encouraging participants to develop algorithms that will predict the former and assess the latter. This job has traditionally been performed by credit officers, among the most valued and skilled employees in a bank, but a group that has often been in short supply. Their scarce skill is now being augmented by machine learning algorithms trained on large datasets of loan size and borrower history that may not only be more accurate than their human counterparts, but will remove unwelcome constraints on a bank's growth.

FishFace and Sustainable Tuna Catch

FishFace is the name of The Nature Conservancy (TNC) project to use machine learning to identify the different species of tuna caught by fishing boats. It uses a variety of computer vision technologies to automate real-time at-sea collection of data on the species and numbers of fish caught, thereby enabling fisheries managers to make evidence-based resource management decisions. The project addresses a perennial problem in fisheries management, the lack of reliable knowledge about the size of catches of target and nontarget species relative to sustainable harvest quotas. Globally 34% of fisheries are now overfished and another 60% cannot sustain any additional fishing pressure.[8] Further, TNC estimates that 90% of all fisheries have no effective management in place.[9] In the absence of precautionary management frameworks and easy ways to verify compliance with regulations on sustainable catch, conservationists fear that fisheries will collapse and this will have disastrous implications for the three billion or so people who count seafood as a significant source of animal protein. TNC's solution is to turn real-time data on fish catch by species into a risk management tool that will allow large operators to validate that their catches comply with sustainability commitments and regulations. This would bring fisheries into line with supply chain verification of sustainability in land-based agriculture.

The catalyst for FishFace was TNC winning the popular vote of the Google Impact Challenge for Australia in 2016. Some of the prize money was used to identify a machine learning algorithm through a Kaggle competition that offered prize money of $150,000. Participants had to predict fish numbers of different species using video data collected from fixed cameras on board fishing vessels. The competition was open for five months and 2,293 teams took part, making this one of Kaggle's most popular competitions.

Participants received a training dataset of 3,792 images and a testing dataset of 1,000 images from the fishing boat cameras. The teams had to classify the fish into eight species, including yellowfin tuna, albacore tuna, dolphin, and shark. A public leaderboard score was computed for results on the 1,000 test images. On GitHub, Felix Yu, who came in third in the public leaderboard stage, highlighted the challenges of crafting an algorithm from the video data, which included only small samples of some species, unclear images of fish fins (an important identifier), and the impact of wave action on the images.[10]

Fast-forward to 2022 and the good news is that the FishFace algorithms have been used on board a fishing vessel in Indonesia with an accuracy of 90–95%, an acceptable level for reporting compliance.

The next step is to develop a minimum viable product that will work on the 100,000 large fishing boats that account for 50% of the global seafood catch.[11] The TNC team led by Mark Zimring is partnering with Amazon's AWS, leaders in cloud computing, to develop an at-sea data uploading solution.

TNC's FishFace is problem solving an issue of global significance, harnessing real-time data capture with a pattern recognition learning engine to crack an age-old problem in fisheries management. It is a great example of the power of competitive crowdsourcing to solve complex problems.

Collaborative Crowdsourcing—Standing on the Shoulders of Others

Where Kaggle and other prize platforms are competitive, and often draw on ideas from outside the ecosystem, open source software development is collaborative, and joins together developers who are mostly inside the ecosystem. Open source software (OSS) development allows large and small companies, new enterprises and behemoths, to stand on the shoulders of others. After roughly 50 years of parallel and interlocking development, we have reached a point where open source and proprietary software are both thriving and have a symbiotic relationship. Big developments in core infrastructure have often come from open source development collaboration, while "last mile" tailored and specific applications have almost always been in proprietary software.

The most famous collaborative software development project, the Unix operating system found in nearly every scaled software system today, has tag-teamed back and forth between collaborative and competitive development since it began in the 1960s. Its origins are in a collaborative project between communications giant AT&T, MIT, and General Electric, aimed at developing a mainframe computer time-sharing operating system that was called Multics. This collaboration generated some good ideas, but AT&T withdrew, and their internal team of Ken Thompson, Dennis Ritchie, and others developed their own related system that they eventually called Unix.

At the beginning of the 1970s the project began to attract attention from outside groups. Normally this might have encouraged AT&T to create a software sales division and to market the Unix system commercially. AT&T, however, was operating under a 1956 consent decree following an antitrust lawsuit, so it began to license the operating system to academic centers and companies for little or no compensation—but without support. No doubt unplanned, that combination of events spawned a decades-long collaborative effort to build out and document the operating system.

One of the licensees of the operating system was the UC Berkeley Computer Systems Research Group, which developed a version of Unix appended with BSD, standing for Berkeley Software Distribution, that had features many users valued. In a funny twist of fate, a second antitrust suit against AT&T in 1983 vacated the 1956 consent decree, and allowed the company to create a commercial version of Unix it called System V. But with expensive license terms, the many earlier collaboratively upgraded versions of Unix continued to be preferred in both academic and corporate communities. One of these was a Berkeley offshoot called the FreeBSD project, cofounded by Jordan Hubbard.[12]

Hubbard sees no inherent conflict between open and closed source software, instead believing they both have a role to play and can coexist.

> *"Writing open source code is a lot like playing in a band. Maybe you have a day job, maybe you just play musical instruments for fun, and occasionally you and your friends actually go on stage. You're not doing it for money, you're doing it because it's more fun to play in front of an audience than just playing in your garage."*[13]

More than a decade after leaving Berkeley, Jordan joined Apple's Darwin project in 2001 to manage its BSD technology group. With its foundation code largely driven by public collaboration, the Darwin project flourished in an open source environment, and the project's kernel still underpins both Mac OS X and iOS to this day, demonstrating the compatible relationship between proprietary and open source development. The company benefits significantly from the previously established community of UNIX and FreeBSD developers.

The past decade has been one of symbiosis between OSS and proprietary software. One example is the Apache Software Foundation, the world's largest open source foundation. Apache is a volunteer community that has more than 490,000 people in its network and has made an estimated $22 billion worth of open source software products available to the public at no cost.[14] Innovations such as Apache Spark, an open source unified analytics engine for large-scale data processing, have grown out of the Apache open source community.

The emerging pattern of symbiosis is for foundational software to be created and made available as open source software, then to have proprietary software built on top. Sometimes these are "last-mile" solutions that involve software tailored to particular customer needs and their mix of systems, cloud migration strategies, and analytic needs. This makes for fast innovation and commercialization. Newcomers like Zetaris are able to stand on the shoulders of others and compete with giants as a result. Open source collaboration, relying on volunteers and without compensation, is messy. But it has created much of the backbone infrastructure that underpins the software we all rely on.

A great irony of the symbiotic story of open source software is that Microsoft, at one time the *bête noire* of open source software (see sidebar), is now the leading contributor to open source projects. Its acquisition of GitHub in 2018 puts it at the center of an open source repository of 73 million developers.[15] Joy's law is at work for Microsoft and many other software enterprises.

Growing Pains in Commercial Software for Personal Computers

In 1976 Bill Gates and Paul Allen, co-founders of Microsoft (and students at the same high school), released Altair BASIC, the operating system they'd built for the Altair 8800 personal computer. Despite being met with overwhelmingly positive feedback from the user base, there was a problem: 90% of users had stolen the software! Gates was frustrated and wrote an open letter to the community.

"Hardware must be paid for, but software is something to share. Who cares if the people who worked on it get paid? Is this fair? Who can afford to do professional work for nothing?"[16]

Gates's experience with Altair BASIC perfectly encapsulates the tensions of the time, the battle to capitalize on the boom of personal computers in an era where "sharing" software was the norm. This tension gave rise to an era of strict licensing and proprietary software, out of which came Microsoft. Soon enough, proprietary software became the norm for commercially produced software on personal computers for business markets.

Collective Wisdom

Ancestral Wisdom: "Right Way Fire"

Imagine sitting in a helicopter in Northern Australia next to an Indigenous ranger feeding glycol incendiaries—firebombs, each about the size of a golf ball—into a machine. The machine drops these mini-incendiaries onto the tropical savanna grasslands below, where they ignite into small fires. In that seat, you would be learning firsthand about a partnership between Indigenous rangers and conservation groups, including The Nature Conservancy Australia, where Rob is a trustee. This has led to the reintroduction of millennia-old fire management techniques into Australia, now adopted as a model for the whole country.

In contrast to modern Western practices of fire management that focus on fire suppression, Australian Indigenous communities have been relying on early dry season burning for tens of thousands of years. Called "right way fire" by these communities, it's an approach which benefits land management and prevents destructive, larger-scale fires. It's a kind of collective intelligence that we think of as ancestral wisdom—historical problem solving solutions that had been ignored or forgotten.

Over 1,000 Indigenous rangers now manage the vast savanna grasslands in Northern Australia, an area of 120 million hectares. The fires they start deliberately literally heal the land, although there are risks. "If we do it wrong, we change the landscape for the worse with wildfires, bringing spear grass back and affecting our meat supply like kangaroo," according to Elder Otto Campion, who has led fire teams conducting early dry season burns for over two decades.[17] He also highlights the impact of early season savanna burning on cultural practices, the environment, livelihoods, and the community.

> "Since (the) creation (of) time we live with fire. For fire connects you with family and country. We cook with fire. We heal with fire in initiation ceremonies. Everything relies on fire being managed. The country tells us the fire season is coming, not a calendar where you mark this day or month. It's the changes in wind, rain and grass growth that we observe that tell us when it's the right time to burn. Our old people said to us 'get that fire right.' We were listening."

Western science complements this set of practices, passed down through the generations, with modern experiments that gauge the amount of greenhouse gases emitted from the savanna, and satellite mapping that shows the extent and intensity of the fires. Carbon credits are generated based on the net abatement of greenhouse gases, compared to a baseline of emissions that occur in the absence of early dry season burns. The Australian government plays its part by registering the carbon credits that are produced, which can then be either sold to the government or on the voluntary carbon market.

Conservationists, meanwhile, celebrate the positive impact on flora and fauna of the carefully managed mosaics of unburned country. These allow birds and animals safe corridors between burns, and promotes plant and seed growth. The rich blend of roles is an extraordinary example of collective intelligence.

Tropical savannas, which represent 16% of the earth's land surface and are present not only in Australia but also in Africa, South America, and parts of Asia, are the most fire-prone vegetation on earth.

The dramatic progress brought about by the reintroduction of early season burning over the past decade is visible in the two satellite image derived maps of Northern Australia shown in Exhibit 4.3. The areas colored red in 2009 are where late and more severe burns occurred, while the green segments are early dry season, or managed, burns. The top section of the chart is a high rainfall zone where ranger teams were in place and carbon projects registered. The middle section is largely Arnhem Land, where Otto Campion's people pioneered the contemporary

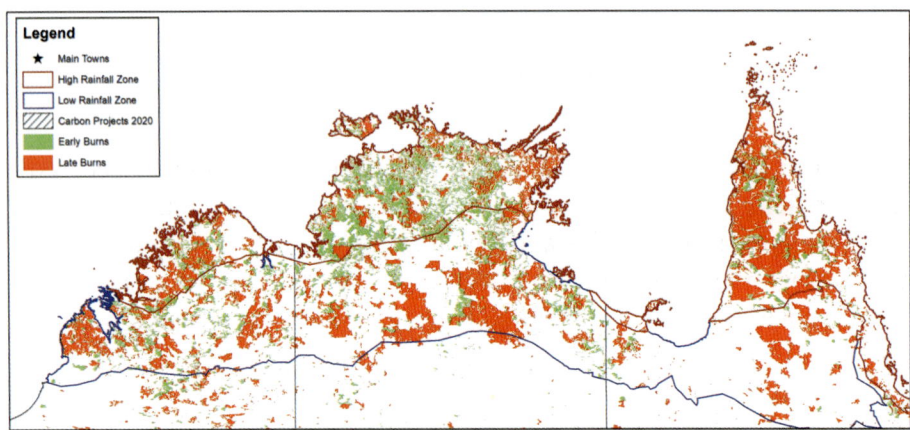

Exhibit 4.3 Northern Australia Fire Scars from Satellite Images, 2009
SOURCE: NAFI, THE NORTHERN AUSTRALIA FIRE INFORMATION SERVICE.

approach to managed fire regimes. The top right-hand segment is Cape York, where managed fire regimes were yet to come into place. In Cape York the low rainfall shows a lot of damaging late season burns, not surprising in the absence of carbon methodology and ranger groups.

Fast-forward to 2021: Wildfires have largely disappeared from the high rainfall zone where traditional burning now takes place (see Exhibit 4.4). It's an extraordinary change in a landscape, probably one of the most significant we are aware of on our planet. The other change is that there has been a sharp reduction in late burns in the low rainfall zone compared to a decade ago. You can also see some carbon projects extending into the low rainfall zone.

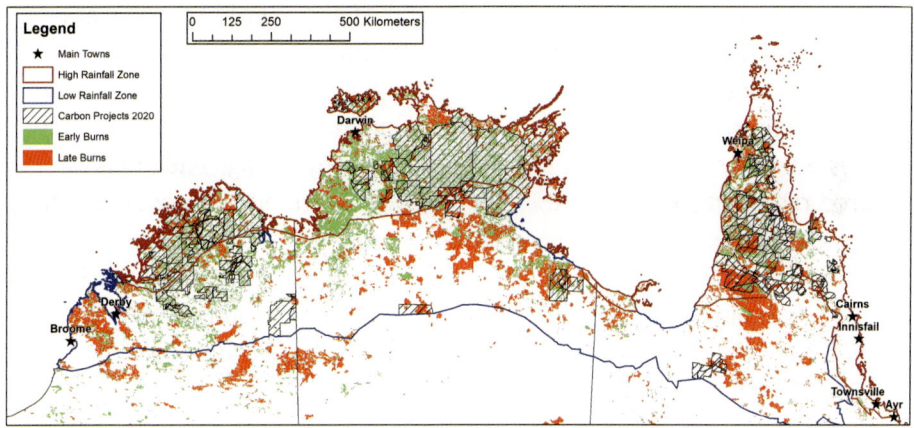

Exhibit 4.4   Northern Australia Fire Scars Satellite Imagery, 2021
SOURCE: NAFI, THE NORTHERN AUSTRALIA FIRE INFORMATION SERVICE.

All this has come about because the Australian government accepted that the Indigenous people who managed this land for millennia should return to their historical fire and land management practices, now in partnership with modern science. The combination is a powerful example of collective intelligence benefiting climate, nature, and people.

AI-Enabled Collective Intelligence

Collective intelligence is increasingly AI-enabled. Geoff Mulgan, author of *Big Mind*, contends that the most successful examples of collective intelligence are hybrid assemblies of human and machine.[18] More and more, connecting humans and machines is part and parcel of problem solving. Mulgan argues that "connecting large numbers of machines and people makes it possible for them to think in radically new ways, solving complex problems, spotting issues faster and combining resources in new ways." However, statisticians like Gird Gigerenzer, who popularized simple heuristics to guide problem solving, implores us not to "equate computing power with human intelligence" and reminds us that the task of "how to teach a neural network to acquire common sense remains an unsurpassed challenge."[19] The sweet spot for AI in aiding collective intelligence is problem solving where conditions are relatively stable, uncertainty is low, data availability is high . . . and common sense is not required.

TikTok versus Quibi

Quibi was like a shooting star you might have missed. A short-form streaming platform launched with great fanfare in April 2020, the company was dissolved on December 1 of the same year. An A-list of investors included Alibaba, Disney, Google, Goldman Sachs, and 21st Century Fox. They invested $1.75 billion and lost over $1 billion in those short months. An all-star management cast was led by Meg Whitman, the former CEO of eBay and Hewlett Packard, and Jeffrey Katzenberg, of Disney and Dreamworks.[20] They were flanked by expertise in streaming content from Netflix and Amazon Studios. This was a team of experts that knew what the market wanted.

How could this possibly go wrong? Quibi failed, in co-founder Jeffrey Katzenberg's words, because "everything about it was swimming against the tide."[21] He believed that COVID-19 undermined Quibi's appeal to 25- to 35-year-olds as consumers were no longer restricted to mobile devices during the day. Quibi was wedded to portable device usability, to charging for content, and to prohibiting the sharing of content. The app was downloaded 4.5 million times during the second quarter of 2020, a promising launch. But by the third quarter of 2020 Quibi had only 710,000 paying subscribers. It was losing 90% of early users after their free trials expired. The value proposition clearly wasn't strong enough to drive recurring revenue.

Quibi's failure—as short-form video content competitor TikTok was rising—had several dimensions. Most importantly, its model of curating content via experts was less attractive than the AI-enabled crowd curation model adopted by TikTok, which reported 315 million downloads in the first quarter of 2020. Indeed, Christian Stadler's post-mortem on Quibi argued that "it failed because executives refused to see TikTok as its biggest competition."[22] What was it about TikTok that made it such a formidable threat to Quibi? The answer is that TikTok embraced the collective intelligence of its users, with a highly sophisticated AI curation of user-provided content, in contrast to the limited expert-driven model of streaming content favored by Quibi. The Hollywood and tech elite were upstaged by a Chinese game company.

TikTok's basic design in 2016 incorporated 15-second videos paired with music, often with a dance or "viral challenge" moment. Young people around the world loved TikTok and began using the platform in ever more creative ways. TikTok's success revolved around the interface experience and consumption of on-demand entertainment micro-curated to the user's specific content interests. This is done through the use of highly optimized AI algorithms that get smart quickly for each user. The AI works through "liked" videos, replayed videos, videos swiped rapidly, and those that are shared with others. Real-time traffic distribution is based on analysis of the user's hashtags, personas, and feedback data, and layered with engagement levels based on audience demographic breakdown. The technology anticipates new trends, allowing an endless and highly attractive video stream by controlling an enticing menu of entertainment.

Quibi could not compete with a social media platform that could pivot to social trends instantaneously, nor sustain a viable revenue model from subscriptions in the face of a service that was free to users and supported by paid advertising. TikTok ultimately created additional revenue streams by transferring users to an online shop site inside the app. It reached 1 billion monthly active users globally in 2021, four years after its launch. By comparison, Instagram took eight years to reach the same milestone (see Exhibit 4.5).

As we reflect on how collective intelligence is evolving, the marriage of crowdsourcing input to machine learning engines is the most interesting development. TikTok is a striking example.

TikTok's battle with Quibi highlights the great divide in problem solving that is at the heart of this chapter. The old model that Quibi employed was fashioned in the industrial era. It involves creating small teams of managers with similar training, supported by technical experts.

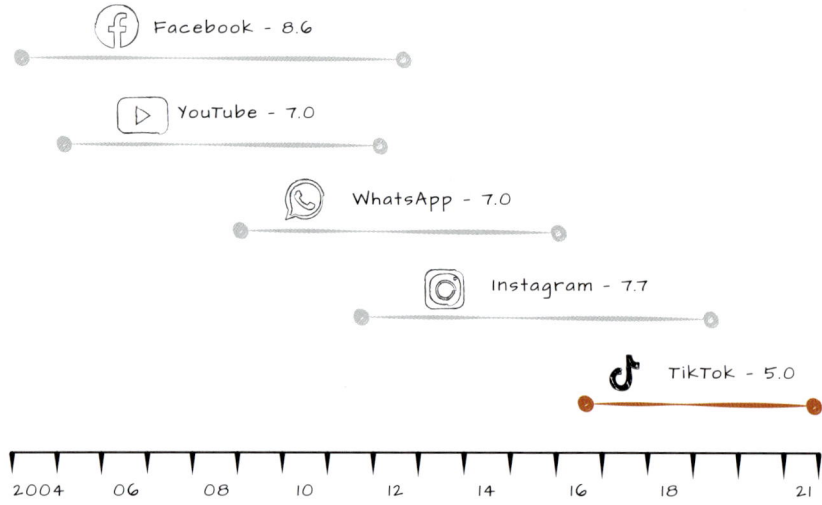

TIKTOK'S METEORIC RISE

Time from launch to 1 billion users; years

Exhibit 4.5

SOURCES: STATISTA; *THE ECONOMIST*.

The new model used by TikTok is characterized by instant learning from diverse customer experiences, and makes full use of the human–machine interface of AI for serving up content. In this new world, accessing collective intelligence is fundamental to competing successfully; old-school expertise is secondary.

AI Swarms

The intersection of individuals and teams who are utilizing tandem human–machine capability is growing rapidly. Take AI "swarm platforms" for prediction. In a contest to forecast the outcome of 50 English Premier League soccer games, swarm participants correctly predicted 72% of winners, while those doing it in ordinary crowds or alone in isolation were correct only 55% of the time. This amounted to a 31% increase in accuracy where participants were connected in AI swarms.[23] The difference between the processes is that participants in swarms "think together" in real time and converge on solutions through interactions governed by algorithms. The swarm process is based on bees, schools of fish, or flocks of birds. A corporate leader in this space is Unanimous AI, which describes a swarm as a brain of brains, able to achieve superintelligent results and outperform all the individual members.

How does an AI swarm compare with findings from deep learning? A study at Stanford Medical School found that groups of doctors using swarm AI algorithms were 22% more accurate in making diagnoses than the most advanced deep learning algorithm that only used historical data. Clearly, having humans connected with a swarm is producing encouraging findings. DeepMind has made significant progress in creating Alpha Code to write computer code at a competitive level, where it now ranks in the top 54% of participants in programming competitions.[24] In the spirit of collective intelligence, DeepMind is putting the dataset of problems and solutions on GitHub to spark innovation in problem solving and code generation.

5,000 Expert Calls in a Minute

A superhard materials company looking for new areas of growth employed an expert-plus machine approach.[25] Superhard materials are materials like diamonds, used for cutting, that exceed 40 gigapascals on the Vickers hardness test. They are typically boron-carbon-nitrogen compounds. The company started with experts so as to establish the right search terms, then unleashed the natural language programming (NLP) AI. The team used the platform of a company called Spark Beyond to identify trends in superhard materials, notably where new patents were being taken out, a leading indicator of where to expect new products. The platform helped the company identify high potential growth areas like nano diamonds. These are diamonds less than 1 micrometer in size that are used in polishes and engine oil additives. Sasha Vesuvala, team leader of consulting firm McKinsey, who assisted with the assignment, expresses the value of the AI platform this way: "Think of it as being able to do thousands of expert calls in minutes. As long as the information is out there, the machine will find the answers because it can read incredibly fast."[26] The outcome of the new product analysis was a faster timeframe for growth, especially important to the private equity owner.

The cases of AI-enabled collective intelligence illustrate a broad suite of problem solving applications. The traditional model of internal teams focused on problem solving has an important role to play, but even the most experienced experts will have their views placed in perspective by readily available swarm platforms.

That said, while AI and machine learning will become familiar tools for collective intelligence, they will not always hit the mark, as we saw with attempts to use them to design treatment protocols for COVID-19 early in the pandemic. We know that when uncertainty is high and data is thin, AI's pattern recognition capabilities are at their weakest.

Collective intelligence from crowds also has its limitations. Todd Rose reminds us of *collective illusions* that occur when individuals subsume their private view to conform with what they think the group wants.[27] An example is the tulip mania of 1835, when tulip prices exceeded their weight in gold. He also points to climate change in the United States, and the gulf between the private view reflected in its ranking as the number-3 most important issue for individuals, and its number-33 ranking when people are asked what the public thinks. The way to avoid collective illusions is to keep asking *why*, as the child in the Curiosity mindset would have us do, and "Is it really true?" to avoid the fate of the Emperor whose (lack of) new clothes revealed all.

How to Implement Collective Intelligence in Your Organization

What if organizations allocated 20% of their innovation funding to collective intelligence solutions such as the Kaggle platform competitions? Or followed the lead of pharma companies in partnering for much of their drug discovery with universities and risk-taking, creative biotech companies? We would most likely see a huge upsurge in innovation as collective intelligence from outside organizations is brought to bear on our most difficult problems. We would have myriad talented people toiling in our gardens, as Bill Joy proposes. Lego's invitation to its millions of users to design new bricks and kits would become a model for new product development. Canada's Goldcorp initiative inviting proposals on where to find gold, having made available their geologic datasets, could become another model for crowdsourced R&D.

Adopting the collective intelligence mindset opens up new problem solving possibilities. And having the mindset expressed by leaders at all levels of an organization will go a long way toward its widespread acceptance. Here are some steps to get started.

1. *Shine a light on major unsolved problems that, if solved, would impact performance or growth.* The pace of innovation consistently ranks among the top priorities of CEOs and boards. Unsolved problems will likely be associated with high uncertainty, to which some forms of collective intelligence are well suited. Ask whether there is scope for crowdsourced expertise by opening up competitive prize platforms, or collaborative industry efforts akin to open-source software development.

2. *Map the ecosystem to identify innovative approaches.* Collective intelligence solutions frequently come from the broader ecosystem of which your organization is part. Mapping that ecosystem often brings new perspectives and capabilities into view. While The Nature Conservancy knew that the electronic monitoring of fish catches was desirable for the protection of fish species, it lacked the capability to make it happen. It was aware of advances in AI and machine learning but unsure whether they offered a practical solution. A Kaggle competition brought a collective intelligence answer with 90–95% accuracy.

3. *Tackle the barriers to collective intelligence.* If collective intelligence isn't playing the role it might in your organization, it could simply be that there are barriers to its adoption. These barriers could be policies on intellectual property or licensing that need to be reviewed to reward innovative solutions, or a lack of resourcing for collective intelligence solutions. For example, following Lego's lead in crowdsourcing new block designs from customers requires resources and teams to respond, assess, and adopt designs. Or a barrier may be a simple bias to innovating the way that has worked before, such as limiting external input to advisory boards of experts. Finally, there is a barrier that lies in awareness of how collective intelligence can aid problem solving, particularly if there is no experience with AI/ machine learning in your organization.

4. *Address the social side of collective intelligence.* Team construction and behavior are vital. Do your teamwork norms encourage open debate,

perspective taking, diverse team membership, and senior people speaking last, not first? Don't forget that "collective illusions" from conformity and groupthink is the flipside of collective intelligence.

5. *Then answer this question: "Do we really have many others toiling in our garden and leading us to better performance?"* The example of Northern Australia, where fire management now utilizes ancestral wisdom passed down from 60,000 years ago, is an inspiration. Only when nonprofits and companies listen to the collective wisdom of their wider communities and broader ecosystems in this way will the investment in collective intelligence have paid off.

Chapter 5
Imperfectionism

Big Bet on Shiny Metal

In 2007, Tom Albanese was only a few months into his new job as CEO of Rio Tinto, one of the world's oldest and largest mining firms. It was a highly uncertain time—Rio Tinto's largest competitor, BHP, had just launched an unwelcome bid to acquire the company. Rio Tinto rejected it, but Albanese felt intense pressure to make an immediate and significant strategic move. He eyed Canada's premier aluminum business, the Aluminum Company of Canada, known as Alcan. At the time, aluminum prices were about $1.20 per pound, a 35-year high, signaling top-of-market risk. Rio Tinto was heavily dependent on iron ore, and aluminum seemed the right metal for the future: light, corrosion-resistant, and used to manufacture a wide range of products, from cars to airplanes. China appeared to be preparing to enter the global aluminum market too, but Albanese reasoned that Alcan would enjoy a sustained advantage from Canada's low-cost hydro-powered electricity.

What to do? The chairman of Rio Tinto, to whom Albanese reported, was rumored to favor the idea of adding another leg to the company's strategic stool. Albanese decided to go all-in and Rio Tinto launched its bid. Unfortunately, competitors Vale and Alcoa had a similar idea, and soon Rio Tinto was in a dogfight for Alcan—eventually paying 60% more than the pre-merger share price, a whopping $38 billion in cash. Given Rio Tinto's market capitalization of only $90 billion at the time, this amounted to betting the firm. To generate sufficient cashflows to service its debt and justify the outlay, the aluminum price would have to hold up, the company would need to expand production, and costs would have to be trimmed. It was the biggest of big bets.

It turned out to be a terrible wager. The world fell into a major economic downturn in 2008, and aluminum prices dropped by nearly 40%. Chinese firms flooded the market with cheap metal. Rio Tinto was left with $40 billion in debt and few strategic options; just as the recession was ending and a long period of economic expansion getting underway, the company was forced to focus on repaying its borrowings rather than growing its business. By 2012, Rio Tinto had written down Alcan by $20 billion, half of its acquisition price, and faced a stark choice: Either dilute shareholders' holdings by raising $15 billion of new equity, or enter into a humiliating partnership with a leading Chinese competitor, Chinalco. In January 2013, the board announced that Albanese was stepping down.

More than a decade later, Rio Tinto's market capitalization had still not regained its 2008 level. It is now the fifth-largest aluminum producer, behind three Chinese firms, and the second-largest iron ore producer, in the world, behind Brazil's Vale. Aluminum accounts for only 19% of Rio Tinto's sales, down from 41% in 2008. The big bet it made nearly 15 years ago still casts a long shadow over the company.

A Mindset for Leaning into Risk

Tom Albanese didn't suffer from risk aversion—on the contrary, he leapt into uncertainty at a time of peak commodity prices with a bet that nearly killed the business. All the indications are that he didn't adequately understand the structure of his strategy problem, the size of the stakes, or the odds of success. In this, of course, he is certainly not alone. History shows that the returns on M&A, particularly transformational acquisitions outside core businesses, are often abysmal. By one analysis published in the *Harvard Business Review*, 70–90% of all mergers fail.[1]

In this chapter we discuss the third strategic possibility between risk aversion and betting the company, stepping into risk as an imperfectionist. Imperfectionists don't wait for perfect conditions to act, but they also don't leap before they look. Perhaps you have heard the aphorism, often incorrectly attributed to Leon Trotsky, "You may not be interested in war, but war is interested in you." Even if your preferred move is *not* to make a move, that nonmove can be just as consequential. You may not be ready for risk, but risk is ready for you. "No plan of operations extends with certainty beyond the first encounter with the enemy's main strength," wrote the great nineteenth-century German military strategist, Moltke the Elder. Champion boxer Mike Tyson put it more succinctly: "Everyone has a plan until they get punched in the mouth."[2] Mike Tyson is an imperfectionist!

The True Costs of Risk Aversion

In breakthrough experiments on decisions under risk conducted in the 1970s, Daniel Kahneman and his colleague Amos Tversky found that people typically weigh losses more heavily than gains.[3] This aversion toward making mistakes was baked into evolution as humans learned things the hard way. But the consequences for human problem solving to this day are profound.

Our friend Professor Dan Lovallo, together with his co-authors, coined the term *risk aversion tax*, or RAT, to explain the phenomenon of risk aversion embedded in corporate hierarchies.[4] The RAT is the difference in value between the choices a manager should favor, based on the odds, and those that managers actually make. Lovallo provides numerous examples of how managers make risk-averse choices even where favorable odds are clear. For example, Lovallo and his co-author Tim Koller presented a scenario to 1500 managers to assess risk-aversion.[5] A proposed investment of $100 million has some prospect of returning $400 million over three years—but all of the investment could be lost in year one. They asked the managers, "What is the highest chance of loss you would accept and go ahead with the investment?" Probability theory says we should require only a 25% chance of success to break even, because a quarter of $400 million equates to the $100 million investment. But the managers surveyed saw it differently, and were only willing to accept an 18% chance of loss. The RAT here is a sizable 57%. And it's not just the size of the bet that drives caution: The researchers got a similar answer when they tried the experiment with an investment of $10 million and potential gains of $40 million.

You might think this is just a theoretical problem. In fact, in one real-life corporate case study, Lovallo found the actual RAT or hidden tax to be 32% of the economic value of all of the investments the firm made that year. Risk aversion in companies and nonprofits is a fact, and it carries costs that are less obvious than strategic moves that go wrong, but are just as real.

It is always exceptionally challenging to develop strategies in highly uncertain environments, especially when you aspire to expand beyond a core business or core competence. Since competitive landscapes are ever-changing, smart firms *step into risk*, initially with modest moves that help the firm understand the parameters of uncertainty in adjacent markets, and eventually with larger moves that build defensible asset and capability positions. They partner to share risk; they hedge risk and lay it off onto others when they can. Related to our M&A discussion, companies that use programmatic acquisitions to roll up adjacent spaces have a much higher success rate than large one-off mergers.[6] We call this framing of strategy development under uncertainty *growth staircases or horizons*, an approach we developed with colleagues a number of years ago.[7] The framework applies to nonprofits just as much as to business enterprises.

Embracing Imperfection

Leaders with an imperfectionist mindset practice humility and tolerate ambiguity ahead of inherently risky strategic moves. They set out to learn, not just to win. They honestly assess past moves and the outcomes that ensued. Importantly, they understand the need to distinguish between good and bad *decisions* as opposed to good and bad *outcomes*, as shown in Exhibit 5.1.

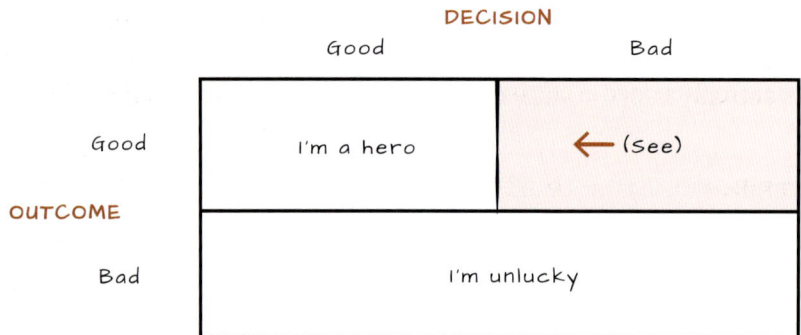

Exhibit 5.1

Most decision makers, however, fall into the trap of confusing good outcomes with good decision making. When we achieve a good outcome, we typically attribute this to great problem solving. When we're hit with a bad outcome, we blame bad luck. This is called the *fundamental attribution error* in psychology literature. Recognize that pattern? Think of your cousin talking about his NCAA basketball finals picks. Even when we try to be cool, detached analysts, it isn't always easy or possible to even know which quadrant in the graphic we landed in after a decision. When we bet on a stock and it goes up, for example, it could be that we had a brilliant insight into the company's competitive position. Or it could be that some entirely exogenous factor lifted all the stocks in its segment (for example, a change in underlying input commodity pricing). In the same way, when we get a bad outcome in a stochastic or uncertain world, it can be that our problem solving *was* good, and we actually did get unlucky.

The trick for developing an imperfectionist mindset is to examine each decision after you know the outcomes. Tease out as best you can what part of the success or failure was due to the way you solved the problem, and what part was due to other factors, such as execution or simply random events. If possible, find a thought partner or partners to assess the decision scenario with you. Was it really bad luck, or was there a factor that you didn't consider in your problem structuring? Critical friends (and good decision processes) are the best defense against ever-present confirmation bias.

Author and financial trader Nicolas Taleb has highlighted the importance of looking at long-tailed and other nonnormal distributions in strategic problem solving.[8] When we model narrow bands and normal distributions for potential outcomes, we can be caught by outlier events. Sometimes excluding these small probability events is reasonable because the costs of maintaining multiple strategies is too high. But unexpected events actually happen quite often. Exhibit 5.2 shows an example from the

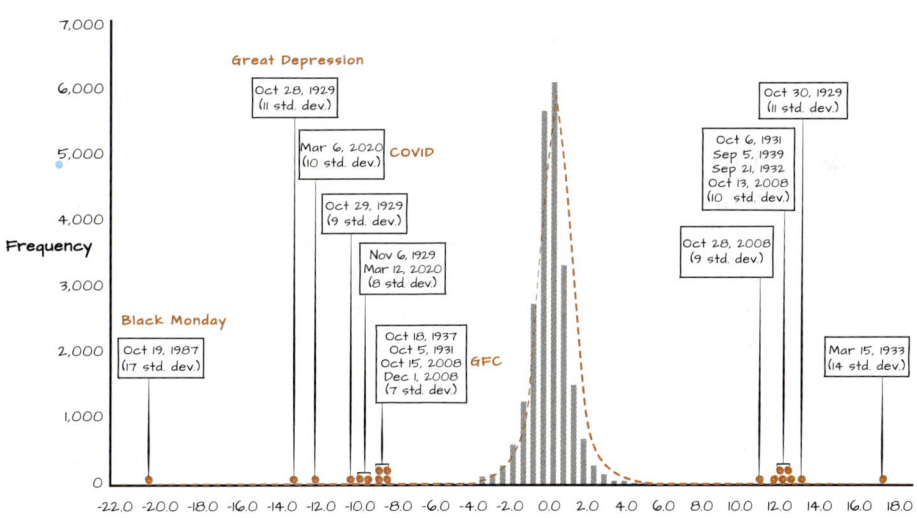

DISTRIBUTION OF S&P 500 RETURNS

December 1927 - February 2022, Daily

Exhibit 5.2

SOURCE: MAKENA CAPITAL MANAGEMENT.

distribution of stock market returns, which shows lots of important events outside the normal distribution.

Decision makers who are open to new learning will better develop a view of structure and probabilities, of how to play the game, and of how to update their initial understanding as events unfold. Annie Duke contrasts *confirmatory* thought, which reinforces ingoing beliefs regardless of outcomes, from *exploratory* thought, which is an open-minded examination of alternative assumptions and hypotheses.[9] Working in teams, especially teams with diverse backgrounds and skills, often encourages exploratory thought. Philip Tetlock has shown that in complex forecasting, teams always outperform individuals, even those individuals he calls "superforecasters."[10]

Framing Imperfectionism Strategies

Robust imperfectionist strategies fall into two broad buckets. The first is a set of moves that helps your organization acquire information and build capabilities to step into risk; moves that improve your strategic position in fast-changing games by smart blocking and tackling; and strategies that allow you to make smart big moves in a sea of risk. In the second bucket are strategies that allow you to pass risk off to others who can more easily bear it, including insurance, hedging, and strategic partnerships. Together they comprise an imperfectionist toolkit that looks like Exhibit 5.3.

Stepping into Risk

Bezos's Bets

Amazon's 15-year expansion into the risky and competitive world of consumer and merchant financial services appears in retrospect to have been a preordained and unmitigated success. It wasn't. The company carefully added knowledge and capabilities through a mix of hiring and acquiring. It eventually built an impressive external, multi-channel e-commerce platform that both serves its core business and is a substantial source of independent revenue. But although the eventual outcome was remarkable, there were missteps along the road. Some organizations view mistakes as failures. But as long as strategic decisions are reversible and reasonable in cost, Jeff Bezos and CEO Andy Jassy empower Amazon managers to make quick decisions and learn from both successes and errors. Each move in a new area, whether successful or not, builds deeper

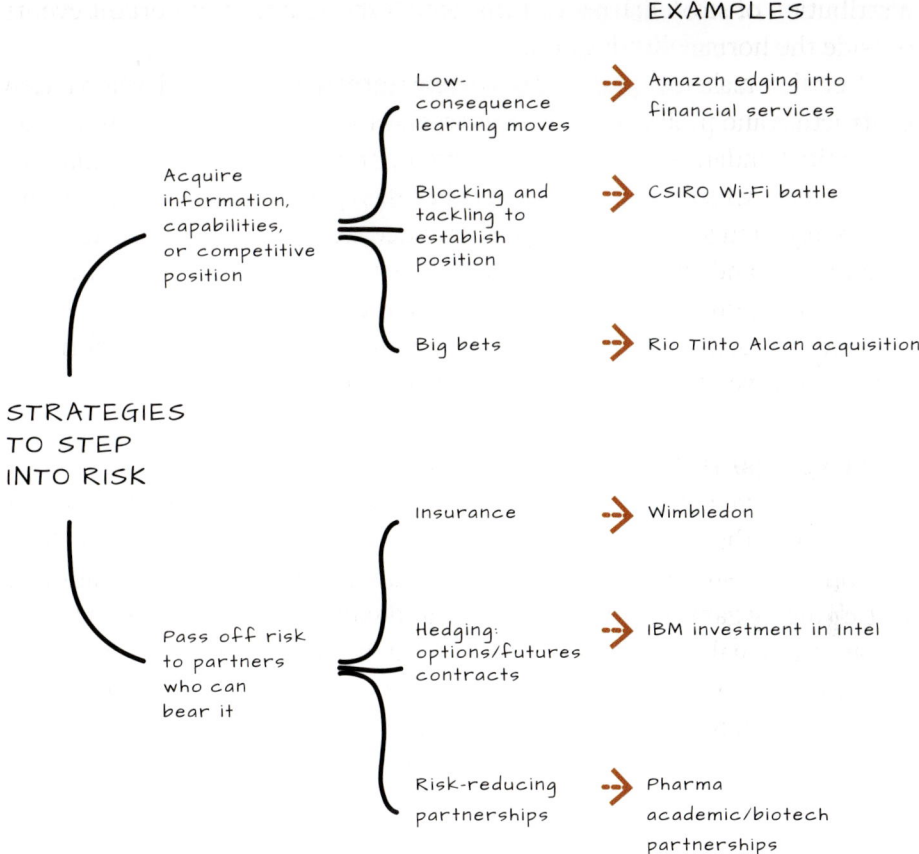

EXAMPLES

Acquire information, capabilities, or competitive position

- Low-consequence learning moves → Amazon edging into financial services
- Blocking and tackling to establish position → CSIRO Wi-Fi battle
- Big bets → Rio Tinto Alcan acquisition

STRATEGIES TO STEP INTO RISK

Pass off risk to partners who can bear it

- Insurance → Wimbledon
- Hedging: options/futures contracts → IBM investment in Intel
- Risk-reducing partnerships → Pharma academic/biotech partnerships

Exhibit 5.3

knowledge of the parameters of risk and the bases of competition. Ultimately, the process builds new capabilities and assets.

With its balance sheet, Amazon could have easily made large acquisitions to build positions in both consumer payments and small business lending. Instead, it entered both the payments and commercial lending sectors through partnerships, the hiring of teams from other ventures, and relatively small investments and acquisitions. It followed a clear trial-and-error approach.

In order to support its core retailing business, Amazon initially set out to help consumers by simplifying payments and providing them with access to credit and cash services. In 2007 Amazon launched "Pay with Amazon," its first internal payments service that built on a core advantage in this area, the one-click payment patent. That same year the company made two other moves. It acquired peer-to-peer payments company, TextPayMe, which was later rebranded Amazon Web Pay. The technology, which was competing with similar independent companies such as Venmo, allowed individuals to send payments to other individuals. Amazon also made an investment in the buy-now-pay-later company Bill Me Later, one of the early players in flexible payments.[11]

Neither of these moves was ultimately a standalone success. Amazon Web Pay was shut down in 2014, and Bill Me Later was acquired by fintech giant PayPal. Another apparent misstep was the launch of Amazon Local Register, a card reader device for small businesses in competition with Square. But the point is that none of these internal launches, investments in start-ups, and small acquisitions should be viewed a failure; they all helped build internal knowledge and capabilities inside Amazon. That knowledge was bolstered by other moves, such as hiring much of the team from failed mobile payments company GoPayGo, as well as targeted senior hires from PayPal, including Patrick Gauthier. Over time you can see how each of these moves built on the previous moves and moved the company up the staircase of competence and position in consumer financial services (see Exhibit 5.4).

Ultimately, these moves put Amazon in a position to launch Amazon Pay, a clever payment platform serving many external retail sites that now boasts a 24% consumer share. To grow this platform rapidly as a service to retailers outside its own site, Amazon agreed to pass on some of its scale savings in credit card processing fees to small and medium-sized e-commerce businesses. Amazon Pay has expanded over time—today it is used for payments to governments, insurers, and for travel—with the result that it is now not only a "sticky" loyalty-building internal service, but a compelling source of revenue for the company in its own right.

As CEO Andy Jassy explained in his 2021 letter to shareholders:

> *"People often assume that the game-changing inventions they admire just pop out of somebody's head, a light bulb goes off, a team executes to that idea, and presto—you have a new invention that's a breakaway success for a long time. That's rarely, if ever, how it happens. One of the lesser known facts about innovative companies like Amazon is that they are relentlessly debating, re-defining, tinkering, iterating, and experimenting to take the seed of a big idea and make it into something that resonates with customers and meaningfully changes their customer experience over a long period of time."[12]*

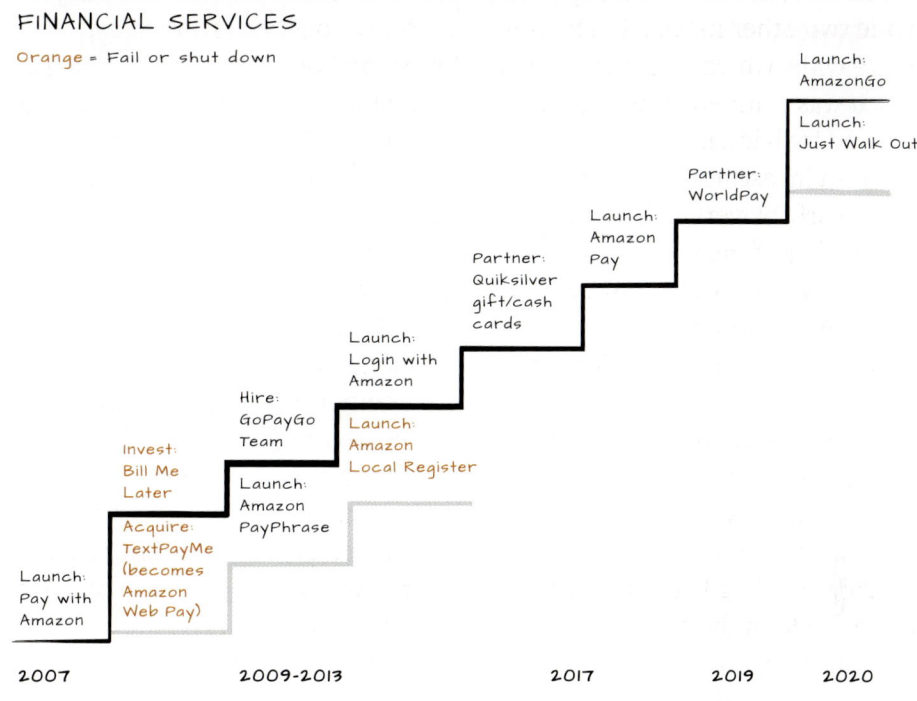

AMAZON'S STEPPED ENTRY INTO CONSUMER
FINANCIAL SERVICES

Orange = Fail or shut down

Launch:
AmazonGo

Launch:
Just Walk Out

Partner:
WorldPay

Launch:
Amazon
Pay

Partner:
Quiksilver
gift/cash
cards

Launch:
Login with
Amazon

Hire:
GoPayGo
Team

Launch:
Amazon
Local Register

Invest:
Bill Me
Later

Launch:
Amazon
PayPhrase

Acquire:
TextPayMe
(becomes
Amazon
Web Pay)

Launch:
Pay with
Amazon

2007   2009-2013   2017   2019   2020

Exhibit 5.4

SOURCE: AUTHOR ILLUSTRATION (INFORMED BY CB INSIGHTS REPORT ON AMAZON 2022).

Knowing "When to Hold Them": Defending CSIRO's Wi-Fi Patent

Negotiations in business have similarities to poker—you're dealt a hand, you play your cards, maybe you bluff or get bluffed. As Kenny Rogers wisely advised in *The Gambler*, "You've got to know when to hold them, know when to fold them, know when to walk away, and know when to run." A small but much-loved Australian government scientific organization, the Commonwealth Scientific and Industrial Research Organization (CSIRO), found it had to "know when to hold them" when it sought to defend a key patent.[13] After an internal review, CSIRO discovered it owned a valuable core patent position in Wi-Fi technology. It could see many large tech companies using its protocol without compensation—the question was how to win the battle to receive licensing fees from these companies.

CSIRO initially committed funding for legal advice of less than $1 million. Attorneys concluded that CSIRO indeed had a strong patent

Staircase Architecture as a Planning Tool

We like to represent strategic development paths through the image of staircases, as shown in Exhibit 5.4. This kind of strategy architecture has three dynamic elements: stretch, momentum, and flexibility (see Exhibit 5.5).

- **Stretch** is the degree to which capabilities acquired as a result of a particular strategic move are new and complex, as well as the amount of effort required to integrate them. Companies need to balance their ability to absorb these new skills with how urgently those skills may be required to establish a market presence.
- **Momentum** is the positive effect of early success, often based in small moves, on the organization's confidence and on its willingness to continue learning. Momentum becomes really important in winner-take-all games, in cases of increasing returns to scale, and where there is strategic standard setting.
- **Flexibility** is being fluid, maintaining option value when uncertainty is high. This can include running more than one strategy (essentially having more than one horse in the race), picking low-consequence choices, and avoiding large sunk-cost options.

An imperfectionist mindset for developing strategies in uncertain environments involves balancing each of these elements as different steps, and sequences of steps, are sketched and modeled. Teams have

STAIRCASE ARCHITECTURE: 3 KEY DRIVERS

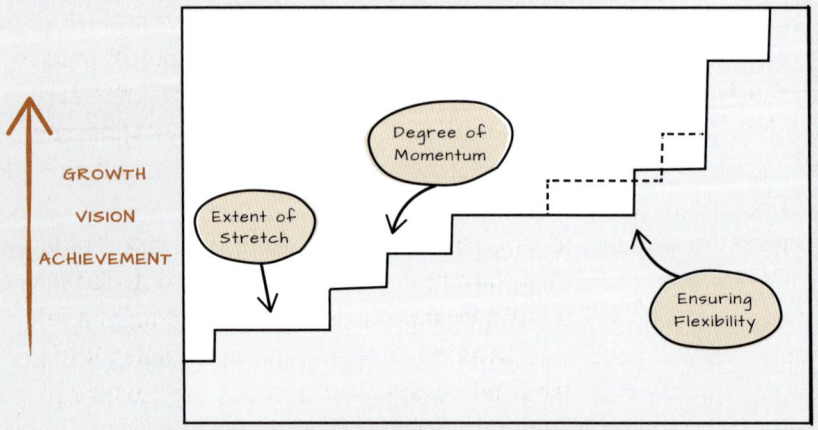

Exhibit 5.5

to debate the trade-offs between smaller and larger steps, which carry more substantial risk. Multiple option-creating moves are attractive in highly uncertain environments, but focused commitments may be a better way to block competitors. Rapid sequential moves can create momentum, but integration with the existing business may become a bigger challenge. Role-playing techniques (such as assigning a "red team" and a "blue team" to make the business case for and against) enrich planning discussion and sharpen decision making. Resources matter. Amazon and Google have made investments in dozens of new ventures. They place many small and large bets in interesting spaces, and often on multiple players in the same space. By contrast, a start-up may have one route to market with no more than a couple of options, constrained by the available venture funding to make a focused commitment.

Staircases allow problem solvers to visualize different ways of exploring an uncertain environment; they serve to focus internal discussion on the stretch, momentum, and flexibility inherent in the choices available.

position to protect, and the executive team and its advisors began to craft a strategy for legal action. Our former colleague and CSIRO executive, Mehrdad Baghai, explained to the board that the cost of the court action was likely to be $10 million, against the value of having their claims upheld in court, estimated at between $100 million and $1 billion. The senior team calculated that CSIRO only needed the probability of success to be 10% to make it a fair bet, and reckoned that the odds were likely better than that. In opening plays that were low-key and methodical, CSIRO informed 28 technology companies that it believed they were infringing its patent; it invited them to enter license agreements in 2003. None was willing to do so. CSIRO had to fold or fight.

Understanding the odds is essential for stepping into risk. To improve the odds, you need to choose *how* to fight, and *where* to do it. CSIRO's next move addressed both. To build legal precedent, CSIRO brought a test case against a single Japanese networking products company called Buffalo Technology, a relatively weak adversary, with a hearing set to take place in the plaintiff-friendly US Federal Court for the Eastern District of Texas. If successful, the test case would create a jurisprudential basis that might encourage other potential licensees to settle. Intellectual property experts knew that the success rate for plaintiffs was 55% in the Texas Eastern

District compared to 33% elsewhere in the United States. This meant that the expected value from the plan was $100 million ×0.55, less a cost of $10 million, or $45 million. This sounds like an easy call, but many managers avoid risky bets even with good expected value outcomes. On February 2, 2005, CSIRO initiated a court action against Buffalo Technology. The board chair Catherine Livingstone felt "it was risky, but the least risky option"[14] (see Exhibit 5.6).

DAVID VERSUS GOLIATH

Wi-Fi patent infringement

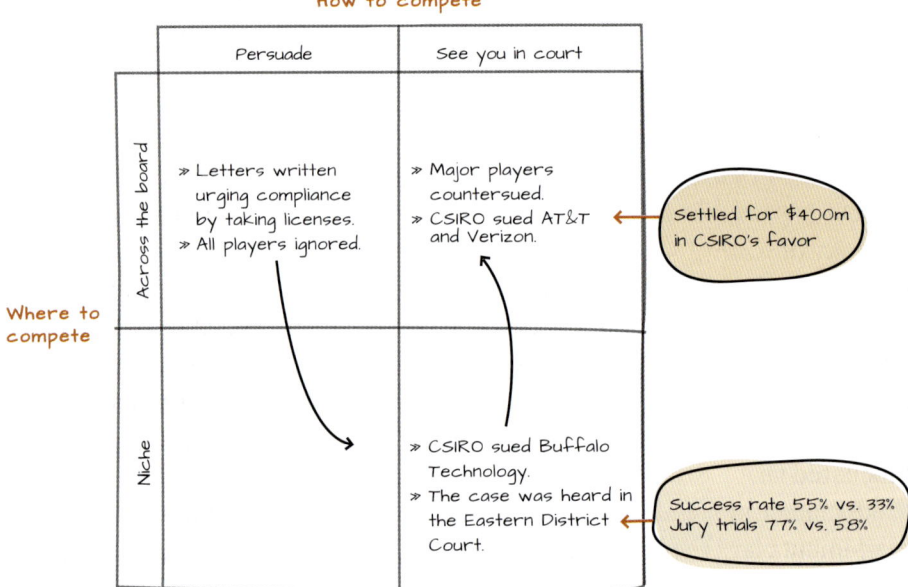

Exhibit 5.6

In May 2005, two separate suits were filed against CSIRO in the Northern District of California for declaratory judgment of noninfringement and invalidity of the patent. CSIRO's adversaries were giants: One case was filed by both Intel and Dell, the other by Microsoft, Apple, Hewlett-Packard, and Netgear. Instantly, CSIRO's costs of defending its patent went up and the probability of success went down, as major technology companies with deep legal pockets tried to move the battlefield to their own turf, the Northern District of California. The *who* and *where* of the fight just got more difficult.

CSIRO was wise to this and moved to have the California plaintiffs' new claim transferred to the Eastern District Court of Texas. In late 2006, the California courts granted that request, consolidating the cases in the Eastern District of Texas Court, back to potentially favorable ground. Also, with budgets tight, CSIRO and its legal team agreed on contingent fees to decrease risk.

The tide turned in February 2007 when the Texas Court ordered Buffalo Technology to stop selling products containing the CSIRO wireless technology. Then, in June, the release of Apple's new iPhone confirmed the vast market potential of Wi-Fi enabled devices, boosting the stakes still higher. CSIRO raised its bet by adding eight additional infringing companies to the legal action, including router companies DLink and Belkin, laptop makers ASUS, Toshiba, and Fujitsu, and game console company Nintendo. In September 2007 Judge Davis of the Eastern District Court requested all 14 parties to attend settlement negotiations, and appointed a mediator to lead shuttle diplomacy between them and CSIRO.

On September 9, 2008, the Federal Circuit Court of Appeals upheld a key part of CSIRO's argument. The trial in the Eastern District court drew closer, scheduled for April 2009. With legal rulings now moving in CSIRO's favor, the pressure was on the technology companies to settle. Hewlett Packard was the first to do so, for $48 million, in late January 2009. Then Microsoft followed and all parties had agreed within a week of the trial's commencement. Things were going CSIRO's way: tackle, block, tackle.

By late 2009, CSIRO had received a significant sum from the settlements—about $200 million. Its legal and executive costs had been recouped many times over. Was it time to declare victory and opt out of this high-pressure game? Not for a smart poker player. CSIRO decided to stay at the table, double down, seek to license as much of the industry as possible to invest further in Australian science. In 2010, with only three years to run on its patent, it prepared a new business case. It upped the ante and sued giant telecommunications carriers AT&T, Verizon, and T Mobile, which sold the majority of smartphones and data plans in the United States. CSIRO also sued laptop makers Sony, Lenovo, and Acer. The case ran from 2010 to 2012 in the same Texas court. It was concluded in 2012 prior to trial for an additional $200 million, when Wi-Fi chipmakers Broadcom and Atheros stepped in to settle on behalf of their smartphone and laptop company clients.

Few high-stakes competitive battles take a decade to play out. This case shows that no matter how well prepared you might be at the outset of a competitive battle, everything changes when it starts (remember Mike Tyson). You have to update constantly your understanding of the game, the stakes, and the odds, ignoring your sunk costs, and playing the next card as coolly as the last one. Blocking and tackling as the game unfolds allows good outcomes for imperfectionists, even with high uncertainty.

Passing Off Risk to Others

Game-Set-Match: The All England Lawn Tennis Club and Insurance

The eyes of tennis fans and players light up at the mere mention of the word: *Wimbledon*. Wimbledon is where *The Championships* have been held since 1877. Wimbledon conjures up the grace of players like Martina Navratilova or Roger Federer gliding over meticulously prepared grass courts. Stalwart fans may also dream of the famous strawberries and cream or Pimm's No. 1, the traditional cocktail served in the bars and restaurants around the "show" courts.

What Wimbledon doesn't convey by its name is that it is a wholly owned subsidiary of the All England Lawn Tennis & Croquet Club (AELTC). The AELTC is a privately owned and exceptionally sophisticated sports management company that generates $400 million of revenue in a typical year. It manages a portfolio of broadcast rights, ticketing, and real estate.

In 2020, when the COVID-19 pandemic forced the cancelation of The Championships for the first time since World War II, AELTC revenue fell by 99%—but it recorded an operating profit of $56 million. How? The Club had taken an insurance policy of $219 million with Lloyds of London to cover event cancelation, with an additional $24 million to be paid in fiscal year 2021.[15] It turns out that the Club had been paying insurance premiums of $2 million per year for 17 years.[16] When the pandemic struck, the Club not only covered its costs, but was able to make modest in-lieu prize money payments to 620 players whose world ranking would have enabled them to gain entry into the Championships. Its hedge, via insurance, against the small but catastrophic risk of cancelation paid off in a big way.

The Club's risk management strategy dates back to 2003. Two experienced company directors, Sir Ronnie Hampel, a former ICI chairman, and Michael Gradon, formerly P&O Group commercial and legal director, formed the Risk Management Committee of the Club's Board. They were joined in 2007 by CFO Richard Atkinson, who had a successful career in media with Time Warner. Between them they had "scar tissue" from unforeseen risks like 9/11, ferry disasters, foot and mouth disease in the UK in 2001, and SARS in late 2002.[17] They brought a passion for understanding risk and considerable experience in implementing processes to manage risk, including a risk register and an annual risk forum.

The Club ranked risks according to their likelihood of occurring and their severity. In this way the committee was able to focus on the *low-frequency but high-severity events* that could affect whether The Championships could be held or not (remember Taleb's long-tailed distributions). One such outlier event is uninterrupted rain over 14 days, which could lead to cancelation of the whole two weeks of play. The board, with input from the Risk Management Committee, subsequently sought to mitigate that risk by investing in a roof over the main stadium so that matches could be played in all weather. The other risks assessed in the annual Risk Management forum included terrorism, cyberattacks, pandemics, and foreign exchange risks relating to broadcast rights. Richard Atkinson notes that pandemic risk came up each year in their forum discussions.

Wimbledon was paying $2 million per year to be covered by a payout of $200 million, an annual premium to payout of 1%, not unusual for an insurable event. However, not everyone was happy. Some members around the board table had asked why they had been spending this money for over a decade without receiving any return.[18]

Perhaps not surprisingly, following the payout after the COVID-19 pandemic, Lloyds of London no longer offers pandemic insurance. Does this mean that the efforts of the Risk Management Committee at the AELTC produced a one-off bonanza? Not in the view of risk practitioners like Richard Atkinson. The AELTC continues to employ a range of sophisticated risk management approaches that reflect the continuing high level of uncertainty, with responses ranging from mitigation to adaptation. Besides insurance, Richard emphasizes the importance of building up what he calls "strategic financial resources" to meet black swan or rare events. This is analogous to banks having high levels of capital to meet a financial crisis. In order to build resilience to risks, organizers of major events like

Wimbledon need to be highly profitable and retain a large share of profits to build reserves. Far from anticipating a return to certainty, they have curated responses to a world of long-tail events.

Revealed Risk

Risk may be revealed through pricing, at least in well-functioning markets. It doesn't mean it's always right, but it is data that may inform decisions and actions. We saw how Wimbledon's All England Tennis Club paid 17 years of pandemic premiums, then cashed in in 2020 with a massive payout on COVID-19. Annual premiums were priced for a 1-in-100-years event. Parts of Rob's hometown of Sydney, Australia, have had four 1-in-100-years floods in two years. This is ample proof to many who have warned of the impact of climate change. For example, there has been a dramatic increase in the risks of living in watersheds, and a repricing of insurance for the 70,000 residents living on the Sydney floodplain. Residents are increasingly forgoing insurance rather than paying the premiums of $30,000 per year now quoted by insurers.[19] Given a likely damage bill from flooding of $150,000, that's a revealed risk of 1 in 5, a long way from the once-in-a-century risk that featured in residents' earlier thinking. Enterprises on the floodplain like turf farms and vegetable farms are looking at altered odds too. If cover is available for damages up to $750,000, the $30,000 premium for them is a 1-in-25 bet. This may be worth considering if you believe a couple of things: one, that the odds of flooding are now more like 1 in 50, and two, that self-insurance involves too high a risk of bankruptcy should a flood happen again in the next decade or so. Prices can reveal risk. Your action depends on your risk assessment and risk appetite.

Hedging Strategies: Invest in Rivals

Insurance is one way to pass risk off to others who may have better resources and capabilities to absorb it. There are also a number of other hedging strategies smart companies employ. Some of these involve the use of futures markets or options to reduce key currency or interest rate risks. Another is taking small financial stakes in early-stage companies that are adjacent but could become rivals, as we saw earlier with Amazon. Other examples include Yahoo's purchase of a 15% stake in Alibaba, which ultimately accounted for more than $40 billion of value to Yahoo—but didn't save the company—or IBM's earlier 20% stake in Intel.

Kymriah: Letting Others Take Early Risks

Big news made its way through the pharmaceutical industry and patient groups in August 2017: the US Food & Drug Administration had approved the first gene therapy for treatment of a childhood leukemia called acute lymphoblastic leukemia (ALL), the most common childhood cancer in the United States.[20] The new drug, called Kymriah, was developed by the pharmaceutical company Novartis in what was then record time—only five years from first patient testing to approval.

It is a remarkable story in several ways. The science is incredible: The patient's own T-cells are genetically modified to include a new gene that produces a specific protein (a chimeric antigen receptor or CAR) that directs the T-cells to kill cancer cells with a specific identifier on the cell surface. The patient results are promising: 83% of the clinical trial participants experienced remission from their cancer. Gene and cell therapies hold the promise of actually curing diseases permanently rather than just treating them. But most of all, Kymriah is a story of clever strategic problem solving in an environment of large and complex risks.

The pharmaceutical industry is characterized by big bets—some of the largest in the business world. Pharma companies invest time and money on drug candidates that fail more often than not. On average, a successful drug takes 10.5 years to move from early clinical trials to regulatory approval, requires upwards of $2 billion in funding, and has only an 8–15% cumulative chance of success.[21] Despite these huge stakes and very long odds, pharmaceutical and biotech companies sit atop the economic return power curve (see Exhibit 5.7).

This begs the question: Why are pharmaceutical companies so successful at managing risk on big bets, earning economic returns well above the cost of capital? Other big-bet industries, like oil and gas exploration, are at the bottom of the power curve. What are pharma companies doing right?

The road to successful drug innovation comprises several stages of discovery: the research stage of understanding disease pathways, identifying mechanisms that affect those disease processes, finding candidate compounds to treat or cure the disease, and then designing and testing of

INDUSTRY RETURNS CURVE - 28 SUB-INDUSTRIES

Average economic profit of companies in industry,
2014-2018, $ millions, n=2,649* in 28 industries

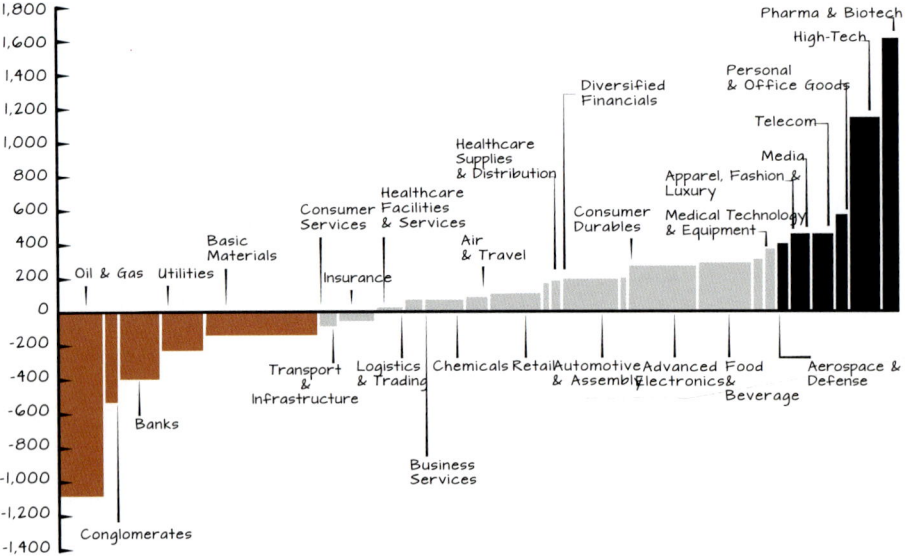

*Largest companies globally where sufficient data is available; incl. financial institutions; excl. private companies and real estate & REITS

Exhibit 5.7

SOURCES: S&CF INSIGHTS, CORPORATE PERFORMANCE ANALYTICS, S&P GLOBAL, MCKINSEY & COMPANY.

targeted therapeutics. The development stage is divided into four phases in the United States: Phase I (small safety studies), Phase II (small-scale efficacy and side-effect trials), Phase III (expensive large-scale studies of safety and efficacy), and Phase IV (regulatory approval and post-approval monitoring).[22]

Statistically, the largest challenge in drug innovation is successfully moving past Phase II, the point in the process where there are the most failures. This is where proof-of-concept is tested in human subjects. Phase II is the stage where the company must decide whether to pursue large-scale, expensive Phase III trials or to terminate the drug candidate.[23] There is a range of reasons to terminate the development of a drug, including commercial viability. Kymriah's probability of success was hampered by being an oncology drug, which has the lowest success rate of the different therapeutic areas—just a 3–5% cumulative probability through all approval steps (see Exhibit 5.8).[24,25]

ONCOLOGY Drugs: PHASE TRANSITION SUCCESS RATE

Percent

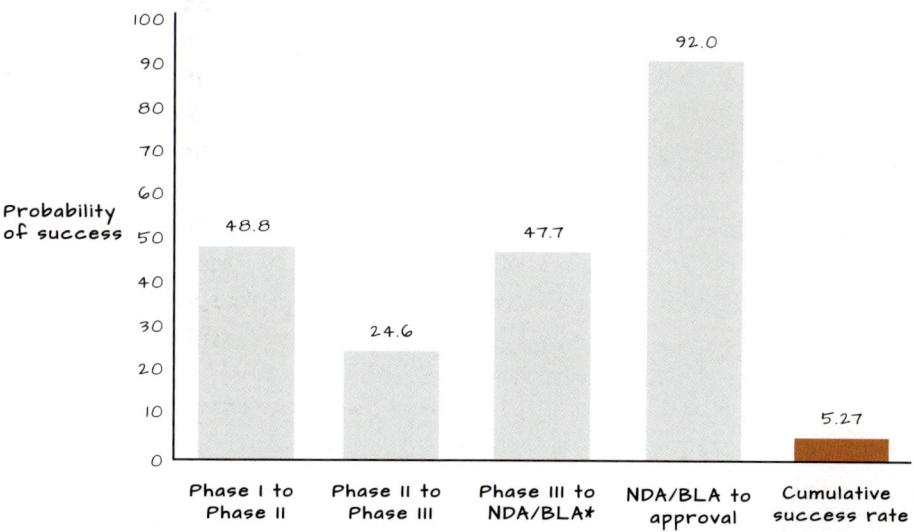

★ NDA = New Drug Application; BLA = Biologics License Application

Exhibit 5.8

Development risk is stacked on top of the earlier discovery risk. But pharmaceutical companies are sophisticated about when to take on risk, and when to offload it to others, including academic researchers and start-up biotech companies. This is their Imperfectionism superpower. Public and private academic researchers, funded by grants, have a higher tolerance for risk, as do the funders of start-up biotechs, which often take early academic ideas and develop them via in-vitro (lab) and in-vivo (animal) research.

In the case of Kymriah, Novartis outsourced discovery risk to the Perelman School of Medicine at the University of Pennsylvania. Under an agreement with the university, UPenn granted Novartis a worldwide license to the technologies it had developed over the previous nine years for treating chronic lymphocytic leukemia (CLL) as well as future CAR-based therapies.[26] Both UPenn and the inventors receive royalty payments.

123

After acquiring the candidate drug from the university, Novartis was able to manage its risks further in the development phase. Usually, drugs must go through a large-scale, expensive pivotal trial as part of Phase III. A pivotal trial is designed to confirm the efficacy and safety of the drug candidate and to estimate the likelihood of adverse side effects. Typical Phase III trials involve hundreds of patients and often cost more than $100 million.

In exceptional cases, however, Phase II studies can be used as a pivotal trial if the drug is intended for treatment of life-threatening or severely debilitating illnesses. In this instance Novartis was able to reduce development risk by accelerating the clinical path through a pivotal Phase II trial with fewer than 70 participants. The company was also able to achieve FDA Orphan Drug designation and Breakthrough Therapy designation, two special programs designed to speed development of breakthrough treatments, which substantially expedited the approval process as well. These regulatory and clinical trials successes with Kymriah enabled Novartis to significantly decrease the costs of development and time to market, and to mitigate risks.[27]

Fully developing a drug in-house represents a big bet that can yield huge payoffs if all goes well, but has a low probability of success. The real Imperfectionism skill of big pharma lies in the savvy ability of its leading players to monitor promising drug candidates residing in academia and small biotechs, assess the risk–return profile of each candidate at different acquisition points, and then move forward when the risk–reward profile is optimal. Alongside this highly developed risk assessment capability, big pharma companies have a substantially lower cost of capital than venture-funded biotechs, giving them natural owner status of outstanding assets. Only 23% of Pfizer's products were discovered in-house, with the rest developed by third parties such as academic centers and small biotech companies.[28]

Bringing Imperfectionism into Your Organization

There was a time when strategy development took place in a planning department, far from operating divisions. The process was done annually and carefully captured in a long document . . . that nobody read. That time has clearly long passed.

Nimble problem solving organizations are constantly developing and testing strategies, usually in small cross-functional teams to whom responsibility has been entrusted. Great organizations don't get disrupted by new entrants because they operate in a constant ferment of imagination, idea generation, and testing, followed by small and large strategic moves.

The best problem solving organizations are humble about their ability to predict the future, but clever about what moves they can make to get more information, develop capabilities, add assets, lay off risk, and build competitive position without betting the farm. That's imperfectionism at work.

A starting point is to ask whether the imperfectionist mindset is in good use in your organization:

1. *Are our decision processes tailored to the problem?* Do we fight both risk aversion and cowboy adventurism by careful assessment of problem structure, stakes, and odds, and then reward smart moves that gather information, skills, and capabilities? Do we separate investment processes into reversible versus irreversible decisions? Imperfectionists push small and reversible capital investment decisions down to frontline decision makers, reserving larger, irreversible moves for the CEO level.

2. *Do we know when to hold them and know when to fold them?* To reflect the uncertainty around you, it's imperative to talk about odds, as we saw in the Wi-Fi case, and to update prior assumptions as the real world unfolds. Organizations that require certainty before they act, or that punish non-company-threatening mistakes, aren't likely to become competitive winners. Not acting can be a sensible choice, but it is a strategic move with consequences like any other.

3. *Is our risk management repertoire right for the level of uncertainty?* Continuing high levels of uncertainty call for a wider risk repertoire than most organizations are familiar or comfortable with. Smart organizations deploy a full tool set and fluently speak the language of options, hedges, and insurance; these are seldom considered outside financial markets, but as we saw with Wimbledon's pandemic risk policy, they are equally applicable in any operating organization.

4. *How do the odds change with significantly more or less funding?* This is the question managers are least prepared for at budget presentations. Managers like to project certainty even at times of high uncertainty. However, if it is possible to estimate the impact of higher and lower funding on the present value of cash flows, a CEO and CFO will have a

better sense for the probability distribution of outcomes and then make better decisions. The enemy of good strategy is a business-as-usual approach that doesn't test the effect of significant resource reallocations.

5. *Learn from pre-mortems and post-mortems.* Part of great organizational problem solving under uncertainty is building a learning orientation into processes. Some organizations do *pre-mortems* before making larger decisions. This is a team forecasting exercise where everybody imagines all the things that could go wrong and that could contribute to a bad outcome. Annie Duke persuasively argues for a related forecasting exercise that she calls *backcasting*, which is the idea of working back from a successful strategic outcome, identifying all the points at which particular supports would need to happen.[29] There is good evidence that these two approaches, *pre-mortems* and *backcasting*, generate different insights into what might work or fail as the uncertain world unfolds.

Chapter 6
Show and Tell

Barry Marshall's Big Gambit

In 1984 Barry Marshall was a researcher at the University of Western Australia in Perth, geographically the most remote city in the world. It certainly felt that way to the young scientist; he had come up with what he thought was a breakthrough idea about the causes of stomach ulcers . . . but he just couldn't convince the global scientific community to take it seriously. Desperate to get his voice heard, he was about to try something crazy to motivate his colleagues to think again about the established science.

Peptic ulcers cost an estimated $6 billion a year at that time, with 6,500 deaths attributed to them annually and nearly 10% of the population afflicted at some point in their lives.[1] Two blockbuster drugs, Tagamet and Zantac, were the accepted treatments, but the limitation of those drugs was that ulcers returned when the patient stopped taking them. The problem for Professor Marshall was that the medical establishment believed that they already knew the causes of peptic ulcers—lifestyle factors, including stress and alcohol—and weren't open to new science.

Marshall's story starts a few years before when his colleague and collaborator, Robin Warren, identified a new bacterium, *Helicobacter pylori*, usually known as *H. pylori*. Marshall says he had no idea what diseases might be associated with the new bacterium, but he nevertheless included a test for it in a study of 100 endoscopy patients. The study results were dramatic—18 of 22 patients with gastric ulcers were also positive for *H. pylori*, and all 13 with duodenal ulcers (those in the lining in the part of the small intestine just beyond the stomach) had the newly observed bacterium, a statistically significant result. While Marshall was sure he had stumbled onto a major discovery, he had to temper his excitement, reminding himself that leading gastroenterologists would hardly accept a revolutionary discovery related to peptic ulcers on the basis of 13 patients from Perth, in faraway Western Australia. "It was just not going to happen," he admitted.[2] The gold standard of trials, a double-blind randomized control trial, would be required.

There had been some recognition of Marshall and Warren's findings in several letters to the prestigious *Lancet* journal in 1983, where they described the new species of bacteria and their findings that nearly all gastritis was associated with its presence. Emboldened by this, and by his successful treatment of four ulcer patients with bismuth, an antibacterial that predates penicillin, Marshall proposed a double-blind trial in which antibiotics would be compared to conventional acid-lowering ulcer treatments. However, he soon encountered a serious setback when the research was funded for only one of the three years that he had proposed—not enough to get the proof. He tried the experiment on pigs, which was cheaper than doing it on humans, but this didn't demonstrate the threshold of proof required. Predictably, Marshall became the butt of jokes among the faculty for his unproven theories about *H. pylori.*

Thirty years old and the father of four children, he was starting to fear that better-funded researchers might get there first. Seeing patients turn up with gastric bleeding, requiring total gastrectomy, injected a new urgency. It soon dawned on him that "the only person who could make an informed consent about the risk of swallowing *H. pylori* was me." Marshall then took a risk—a big risk—to demonstrate his thesis. In July 1984 he underwent an endoscopy of his stomach to obtain healthy control tissue, but didn't explain to the technician that this was his baseline sample. Then he put some *H. pylori* in alkaline peptone water in a 200 ml beaker and drank it, remarking that it tasted like swamp water. He monitored his condition, noticing that from days 5–8 he felt nauseous; at one point he was told that he had halitosis.[3] He had a follow-up endoscopy on day 10, which showed the presence of the bacteria. Only then did he tell his wife Adrienne what he'd done! He scheduled another endoscopy on the 14th day. Although this pathology was clear, he terminated the experiment and took a course of antibiotics for safe measure.

Reactions to Marshall were at times hostile: One Texas colleague called him a real cowboy, another unethical. But his apparent recklessness paid off. Shortly afterwards he was able to get renewed funding and to proceed with a proper clinical trial, the findings of which confirmed his earlier work, along with confirmative studies in Holland, Houston, and Vienna. In 1994 the US National Institutes of Health finally concluded that the first step in treating peptic ulcers was the identification and eradication of *H. pylori*. As Marshall explains, "My key insight was that if all ulcers had the bacteria, it must be nigh impossible to have an ulcer if the bacteria were not there. So, antibiotics must be a cure for ulcers . . . QED."[4] For this work he and Robin Warren were awarded the Nobel Prize in 2005, more than two decades after his *very personal* experimental work.

Storytelling Is a Core Problem Solving Mindset

Facts and data can be richly compelling. No one loves a good data table more than we do. In our companion book, *Bulletproof Problem Solving*, we show the power of data, analytics, and logic in cracking even the toughest problems. But the purpose of great problem solving is to generate an impetus to action, not to look clever. We all would like to believe that compelling facts and logic are enough to motivate change. But they aren't. For one thing, people are overwhelmed with information of every kind—there is now more data produced every one or two days than in the whole history of humankind before the twenty-first century.[5] Furthermore, many people are justifiably hesitant to trust plain facts when so much deliberate misinformation is flying around. We need trustworthy and credible storytelling to compel action in the world as it is.

As we saw with Barry Marshall, even in science—where the core principle of the scientific method is to test theories by challenging them with data—information that contradicts established wisdom is often swept under the metaphorical rug. It is often described as an outlier, or attributed to mistakes in experimental practice.[6] Philosopher of science Thomas Kuhn wrote about this in his seminal work, *The Structure of Scientific Revolutions*. Kuhn noticed that science has a culture just as strong as any physical community, and just like those conventional cultures it hangs on to its beliefs tenaciously. He demonstrated how it often takes a substantial body of counterfacts and countertheory to challenge and then break through the thick crust of a previous scientific paradigm. "Normal science, the activity in which most scientists inevitably spend almost all their time," he wrote, "is predicated on the assumption that the scientific community knows what the world is like . . . [It] often suppresses fundamental novelties because they are necessarily subversive of its basic commitments."[7]

This is true even of the greatest discoveries: Until a scruffy fellow called Einstein from the Bern patent office turned up, the physicists of the era believed that they had solved all the major issues of their science.

Young management consultants learn early on in their careers how challenging it can be to make a compelling case for change. Delighted with a set of sparkly slides highlighting the results of their brilliant machine learning model, or a multivariate statistical analysis, they are often taken aback by the skeptical and world-weary reactions of certain clients. These clients think they know everything there is to know about their business, and naturally resent the whippersnappers sent in by head office. As we mentioned in the Introduction, we used to call this sort of presentation to a skeptical audience *the anxious parade of knowledge*, or APK for short.

Later, of course, these same consultants are trained—just like good journalists—in the pyramid principle for constructing compelling arguments, which looks like what's shown in Exhibit 6.1.

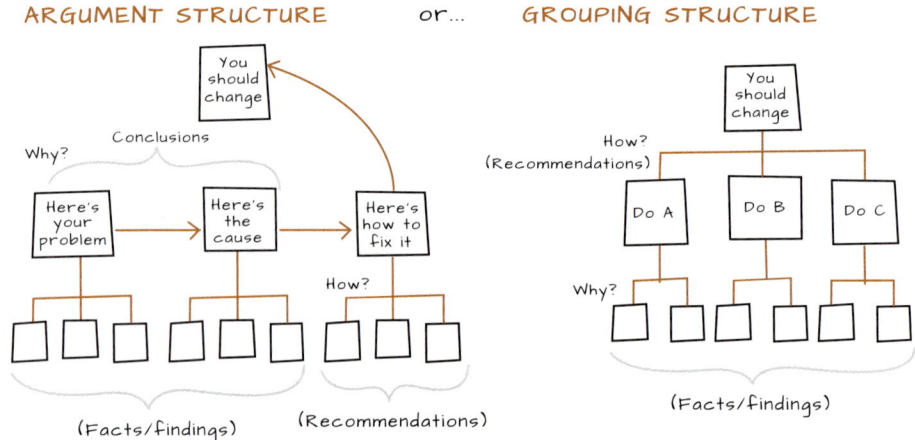

Exhibit 6.1

Don't get us wrong. It's a terrific idea to organize your problem solving results into a governing thought, supported by a logical argument structure, which in turn is supported by analysis and facts. But over many years of practice we have learned that good arguments supported by good facts are simply not enough. To motivate action, to make change in the world, you need to recognize that humans are visual learners, you need to tickle their curiosity, surprise them, speak to their values, and even shock them. Imagine David Attenborough's *Life on Earth* without the video!

Framing Show and Tell

We call this final mindset Show and Tell, and it is integral in driving others to act. We like the fact that the term conjures up children demonstrating their mastery in a classroom with fellow students and proud parents. This mindset amplifies our other mindsets, highlighting a surprising counter-factual from curiosity, showing how a problem looks through a different lens, or underscoring a novel perspective sourced via collective intelligence.

We can organize this into a simple graphic, shown in Exhibit 6.2

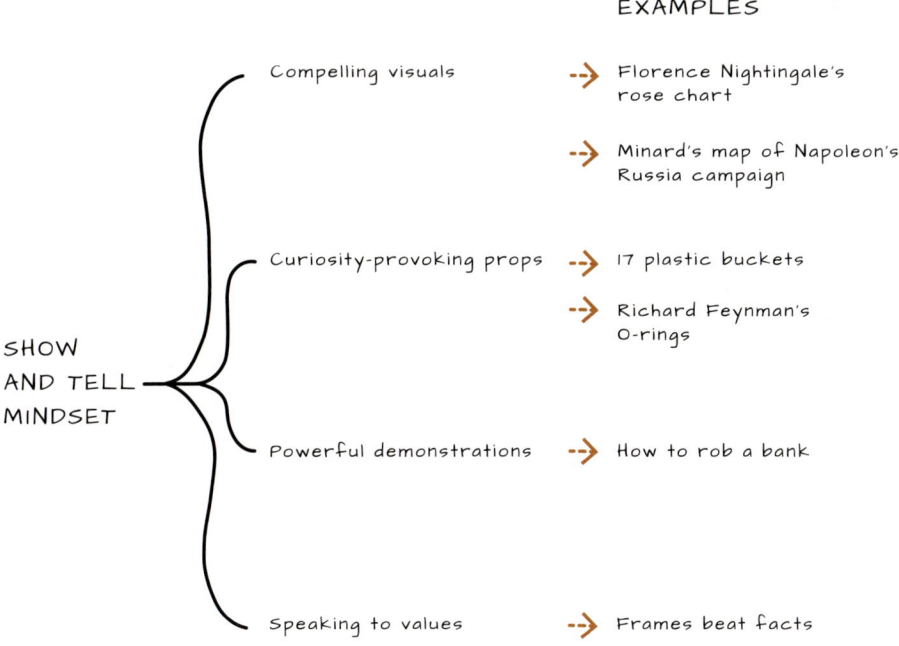

EXAMPLES

SHOW AND TELL MINDSET

- Compelling visuals
  - → Florence Nightingale's rose chart
  - → Minard's map of Napoleon's Russia campaign
- Curiosity-provoking props
  - → 17 plastic buckets
  - → Richard Feynman's O-rings
- Powerful demonstrations
  - → How to rob a bank
- Speaking to values
  - → Frames beat facts

Exhibit 6.2

Pictures Tell Stories

Florence Nightingale, Statistician

Florence Nightingale's name is synonymous with modern nursing, thanks to her role in the Crimean War in the mid-nineteenth century. What many people don't know is that she was also a first-class statistician, and was the first woman elected to the Royal Statistical Society of the United Kingdom. Alongside her legacy of turning nursing into a proper profession, she made enduring contributions to the saving of lives in hospitals through proper collection of data, analysis, and presentation of statistics.

In 1854 Nightingale headed a group of nurses sent to Constantinople (now Istanbul) to provide care for British soldiers wounded in Crimea. The hospital conditions she encountered were horrific, but the male army doctors she came across did not welcome her ideas for improvement. Nightingale famously calculated that the mortality rate of wounded soldiers who stayed at a field hospital at the front was 12.5%, whereas a soldier transferred to the Scutari hospital in Constantinople where she was working at the time had a 37.5% chance of dying.[8] In 1855 a Sanitary commission arrived at Scutari to improve standards of cleanliness, including the repair of sewers and the removal of dead rats. The mortality rate fell to 20% after the changes were made.

In an era when women were not taken seriously in many spheres of endeavor, Nightingale's innovative data visualizations were shocking. They demonstrated with great clarity that the number of soldiers who died of disease before Sebastopol (the siege lasting from October 1854 to September 1855) was seven times higher than the number killed by the enemy.[9] She showed the causes of death month by month in color wedges that represented estimates of the numbers who had died from different causes. These became known as Rose diagrams, sometimes called Coxcomb charts, a form of circular histogram[10] (see Exhibit 6.3).

Nightingale's graphic showed the contrast between two periods, April 1854 to March 1855 (on the right), before the Sanitary Commission visit, and April 1855 to March 1856, after the visit (on the left). Her visualization starkly demonstrates two critical points: first, how much greater were the causes of death from preventable disease than deaths from battle wounds in both periods; and second, how actions to improve sanitary conditions

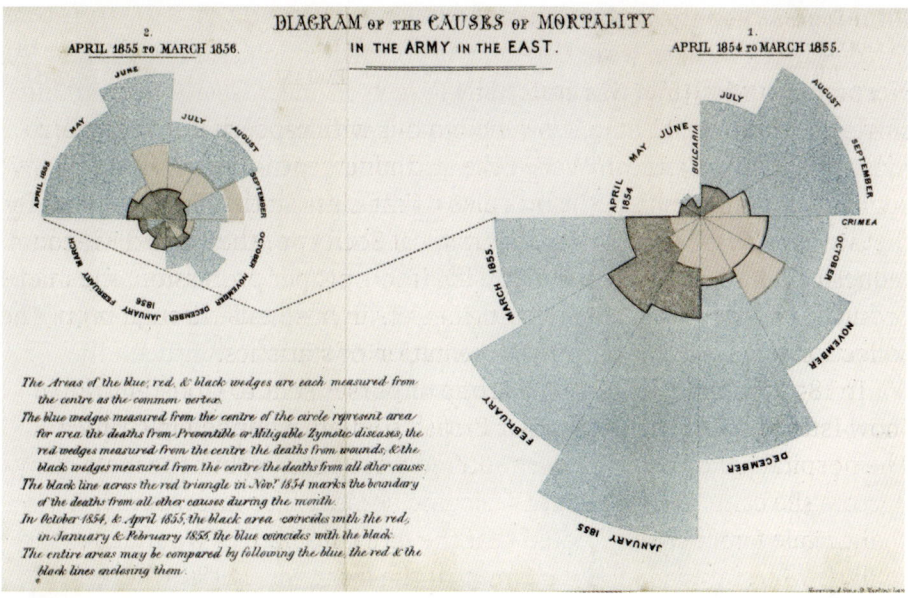

Exhibit 6.3

SOURCE: FLORENCE NIGHTINGALE, "DIAGRAM OF THE CAUSES OF MORTALITY IN THE ARMY IN THE EAST" (1858), ACCESSED ON WIKIMEDIA COMMONS.

led to substantially fewer deaths from preventable conditions in the latter period.

This work had a huge impact on the practice of public health and catapulted Nightingale into the public eye. She is believed to have convinced Queen Victoria to support a Royal Commission on the health of the army.[11] A warrant for the Royal Commission was issued in May 1857 and the report made available three months afterwards. Two decades later the Public Health Act of 1875 required local authorities for the first time to implement uniform sanitary standards.

The story of Florence Nightingale illustrates how a single graphic or picture can capture the public's attention and generate more impact than a million words. PowerPoint may be a necessity of modern corporate life. If it didn't exist, you would probably have to invent it. But it is fundamentally limiting. Think about how you can develop graphics that tell stories as compelling as Nightingale's on public health, and how to bring them to life.

Napoleon's Disastrous Invasion of Russia in 1812

As you can tell by now, we are great lovers of killer graphics. Perhaps the most famous of all time was created by French engineer Charles Minard. In a single brilliant map, Minard showed both the path Napoleon's army took to Moscow and, via the width of the column, the size of his army on both its approach (in brown shading) and on its terrible retreat (in black shading). By the end of the campaign, the French army of nearly 700,000 men had been reduced to a thread, with some three quarters of Napoleon's force either dead or having deserted as a result of cold, hunger, disease, and enemy attacks. The temperature scale at the bottom of the map shows just how difficult the conditions were on the return journey. Minard's brilliant graphic, shown in Exhibit 6.4, captures the entire disastrous campaign in a single picture.[12]

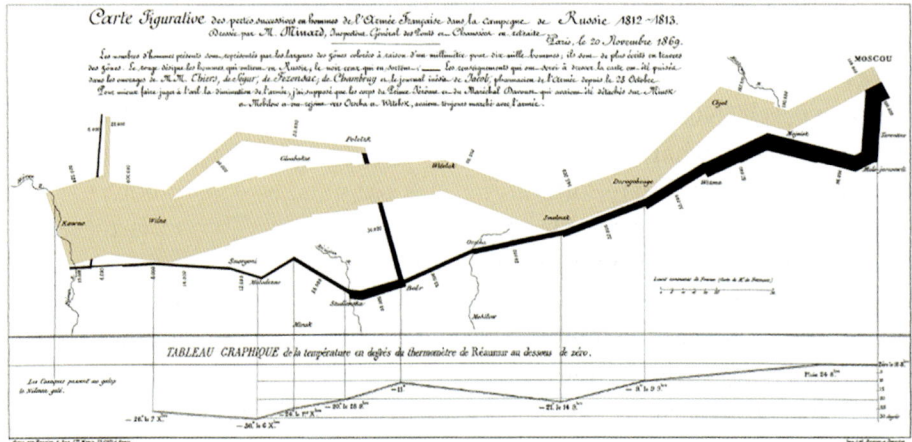

Exhibit 6.4
SOURCE: CHARLES MINARD, 1869, VIA WIKIMEDIA COMMONS.

Spark Curiosity with Props

What Are the Buckets For?

Consider the picture shown in Exhibit 6.5 of 17 green buckets stacked on a sideboard in the boardroom of a major Australian bank. This was the sight greeting executives of the National Australia Bank (NAB) Foundation, the philanthropy arm of one of the country's big four banks, as they filed in to hear a presentation from The Nature Conservancy (TNC) Australia. The unmistakable expression on all their faces as they sat down was *What's*

Exhibit 6.5
SOURCE: RICH GILMORE, FORMERLY TNC AUSTRALIA.

going on here? TNC's pitch was for funding to restore bays and estuaries in South Australia, where a new 20-hectare reef was up for consideration, so it was not unnatural that Foundation staff should be curious about the stack of empty buckets. "We'll explain shortly," the TNC country director replied, knowing his answer would pique their interest.

The presentation described how the ecosystem of bays and estuaries in Australia had become ecologically endangered over the past 100 years, in many cases due to the removal of limestone in oyster reefs for use as road base. The Nature Conservancy team went on to explain how it could restore them, describing the marine work already underway in Port Philip Bay, a suburb of Melbourne in the state of Victoria. This work included a partnership with a local angling and yachting club, the Thomas Foundation, the Victorian government, and local seafood restaurants, all playing a role in bringing back healthy oyster reefs to the Bay.

Reef building, replicated in over 50 locations in the United States including Chesapeake Bay, is a relatively straightforward exercise. At Port Phillip Bay, a barge takes limestone to a reef site about as big as a large football stadium. Then cured oyster shells, saved from local restaurants, are deposited on the limestone. The final step is to put one million oyster spats (larvae) onto the reef site and let nature take its course; in five to seven years you have a reef teeming with fish and marine life.

The benefits of reef restoration are twofold. The primary advantage is that it cleans up waterways, as each oyster filters 170 liters of water a day. The second and more visible benefit is the restoration of normal ecosystem functions, including fish populations. Oysters filter nitrogen from agricultural fertilizer runoff into the bay water; left unchecked, excess nitrogen chokes the system with algae overgrowth. The presentation team's crowning statistic was that these 170 liters per oyster are the equivalent of 17 buckets of water per oyster per day, hence the significance of the 17 buckets on display on the board room sideboard!

By being there as a visual prop they helped Foundation executives grasp the extraordinary work of oysters in filtering nitrogen in bays and estuaries. The buckets could have been seen as gimmicky but played an important role in bank foundation staff being able to visualize the role of oyster reefs in natural system restoration. "It was like an icebreaker that lifted the mood in the room. It brought energy and purpose to our presentation," a TNC team member explained.[13] And most importantly, of course, TNC Australia got the funding it needed to begin work.

Finding ways to grab and sustain attention—using props to deliver a compelling show and tell—can be the difference between a good or a disappointing outcome. This is especially so in the era of PowerPoint and Zoom when it's so easy for participants to switch off mentally in mid-presentation.

It Was the O-Ring That Failed

At a public hearing of the Presidential Commission into the 1986 Space Shuttle *Challenger* disaster, an accident that took the lives of seven astronauts, Nobel Laureate Richard Feynman waited impatiently for his turn to speak. When it came, to the surprise of the Commission and to the television audience watching, Feynman performed a remarkable live experiment (see Exhibit 6.6). "I took this stuff [rubber] that I got out of your seal, and I put it in ice water [here he dunks the O-ring in his glass of ice water] and I discovered that when you put some pressure on it and then undo it . . . it doesn't stretch back . . . there is no resilience in this material when it is at a temperature of 32 degrees. I believe that has some significance to our problem."[14] Indeed it did.

On the morning of *Challenger*'s launch, there were icicles on the launchpad and the temperature at the site was 31 degrees Fahrenheit. Previous launches had taken place in temperatures ranging between 53 and 81 degrees Fahrenheit. Professor Feynman demonstrated that outside this normal temperature range, the O-rings were stiff and did not seal.

Exhibit 6.6   Feynman at Presidential Commission
SOURCE: FEYNMAN.COM.

In the days preceding the hearing, Feynman had met NASA staff to try to understand the causes of failure. He became aware during these conversations that O-ring failures had occurred on previous missions, yet internal NASA reports stated that "analysis of existing data indicates that it was safe to continue flying."[15] That conclusion was simply incorrect, since the damaged O-rings had all occurred on previous flights with calculated joint temperatures of between 53 degrees and 75 degrees Fahrenheit. NASA staff estimated that the probability of failure of the O-rings was approximately 1 in 100,000—Feynman found that the conditional probability was more like 1 in 100 (see Exhibit 6.7).

Feynman was aware that rubber used in the O-rings would be on display at the Commission meeting in a model of one of the joints. All he needed was a pair of pliers to get the rubber out of the joint, and a small C-clamp to put pressure on the O ring. He bought these items at a hardware store near his Washington hotel, and waited for his turn to speak with one in each pocket and a glass of ice water in front of him.

FLIGHTS WITH DAMAGED O-RINGS AND TEMPERATURE

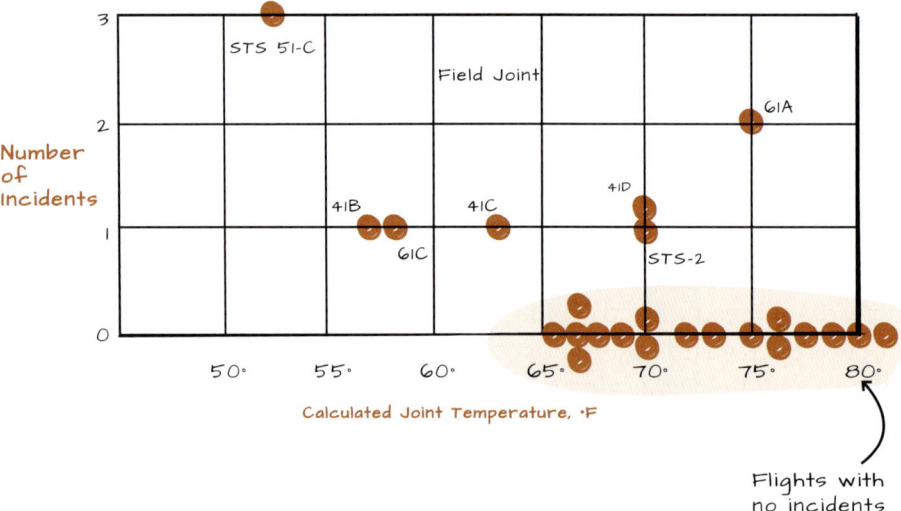

Exhibit 6.7

    The Report to the President on the Space Shuttle Challenger Accident was publicly released in June 1986. It concluded that the disaster was caused by failed O-rings that led to "the destruction of the seals that are intended to prevent hot gases from leaking through the joint during the propellant burn of the rocket motor."[16] That conclusion had been foreshadowed months earlier by Richard Feynman's memorable show and tell. Feynman could have made his points verbally but they would have lacked the dramatic intensity of the real-time experiment he conducted on live television.

When All Else Fails, Use Demonstrations

Robbing the Bank

Two of our most brilliant colleagues at McKinsey were Ted Hall and Don Watters. Working as advisers to the Federal Reserve Bank in San Francisco, they became aware of weak security around the building that housed the vault where all the money is. Don Watters recounts, "We noticed that the bulletproof glass door on the guard shack seemed to be propped open with a fire extinguisher [we later found out that this air-conditioning unit was down for repairs]. After observing the same situation every evening for over a week, we began to be concerned about the Bank's security."[17]

As was typical then, the security staff were older ex-police and military veterans, armed only with handguns. Hall and Watters couldn't convince the senior team that their anxieties were justified, so they conspired with the bank president, John Balles, to stage an actual robbery.

With the senior team observing at close quarters, Hall and Watters got into the bread truck that delivered food every day to the loading dock of the bank—the same loading dock they used for moving currency. Here is how Don described it: "All three of us jumped out from behind the Kilpatrick's Bread van sitting in the driveway, raced up the stairs past the propped open guard shack door (one guard 'down') and headed into the Bank (two more guards 'down') and straight downstairs into the vault." Ted Hall, Don's partner "in crime," continues:

> *"All the way in the back of the secure area around the vault, we knew there was an emergency exit to the street above. And we knew that there was a pair of bolt cutters someone had stored there to allow vault workers to escape in case of an emergency in the secure area. We went back there, back behind the furnace. We found the bolt cutters."*[18]

The Fed's security team—who weren't in on the demonstration—arrived with the San Francisco police department, guns drawn. Don says, "They found bank president Balles with arms crossed standing in front of his two co-conspirators, blocking the first responders' entry to the vault, Ted guarding the three filled-to-the-brim laundry carts, and my arms reaching up to the ceiling with the bolt cutters on the elevator padlock—ready to make the cut." Tensions quickly eased, but the point was made.

Ted and Don's dramatic demonstration led to huge changes in security at the Federal Reserve, from how deliveries were made, to the control of entrances, to access to the loading area. No amount of words would have had the same impact on the bank's management team as the staged robbery.

Speak to Values

Frames Beat Facts

Our problem solving training gave us an unswerving faith in facts, and a conviction that, when presented with these facts and our analysis of them, clients would adopt our recommendations. We often employed show-and-tell techniques like the demonstrations described above to further convince audiences to take action.

That approach typically works pretty well with top leadership teams in companies and in nonprofits. But in the broader world of public policy, where good problem solving is arguably even more important, there is often a fundamental disagreement about the facts. This always reminds us of a favorite *New Yorker* cartoon, shown in Exhibit 6.8.

Exhibit 6.8
SOURCE: THE NEW YORKER (1977).

Psychologist George Lakoff came up with the idea of *frames* as a useful way to help resolve arguments in situations where people disagree about the facts. Lakoff puts it this way: "If we tell people the facts, since people are basically rational beings, they'll all reach the right conclusions. But we know from cognitive science that people do not think like that. People think in frames. If the facts do not fit a frame, the frame stays and the facts bounce off."[19] Lakoff suggests constant reframing in contested situations—every issue every day—and stresses the importance of understanding the values held by participants. Moral psychologist Jonathan Haidt makes a similar point that "people bind themselves into political teams that share moral narratives. Once they accept a particular narrative, they become blind to alternative moral worlds."[20] So much for the facts. To find and communicate effective solutions you have to frame values in a way that all parties can sign on to.

Armed with the insight that frames may trump facts in the policy arena, how do you make persuasive show-and-tell stories? Here we can learn from Katherine Hayhoe, climate scientist, mother, and chief scientist at The Nature Conservancy, who is a tireless advocate for solutions to fight climate change. As a scientist, Hayhoe has a great regard for facts. But she also knows that facts aren't everything. Her framing starts with "who you are and why you care" about climate change.[21] In a LinkedIn post, for example, she has shared the fact that 83% of mothers believe in climate change, common ground for a large and important segment of the population. The common value here, embraced widely across different political perspectives, is the concern of parents for their children's future. This shared value provides an opportunity to build bridges between those who have different beliefs, to share stories, and to develop solutions with a common narrative. To convince others, we need to understand what they value, and tie solutions to the achievement of those values.

Emotion and action are critical elements of effective storytelling, no matter what culture. In classical Chinese, for instance, there are six different expressions for persuasion and a more holistic view of emotion and reason. Our favorite is "self-example persuasion," which means that your own actions are the key drivers of influence over others, as we saw with Nobel Laureates Richard Feynman and Barry Marshall.[22]

Bringing Show and Tell to Your Organization

You may not be ready for your chief scientist to self-experiment with a new medication, or for a board member to conduct a consequential experiment in front of regulators. But there is a full repertoire of show-and-tell ideas that can fit many occasions.

1. *Make an inventory of how and when you can use show and tell in the organization.* Your list will most likely include product launches (think the launch of the iPhone immortalized by Steve Jobs), staff training sessions, and strategy discussions. But it's not just big events where show and tell plays a role. There are many smaller occasions when this mindset can shift thinking in powerful ways. Take board engagement, for example: To understand better the role of people at the frontline helping the country recover from Australia's 2019 bushfires, a philanthropic board where Rob is a director held a working session with Kerrie and Kim, two women volunteers in a fire-ravaged community. These frontline workers had identified the survivors, secured shelter, and found food for those who had been made homeless. Their story was strikingly raw and passionate, highlighting community resilience at its best. The board responded animatedly to the session, captivated by the power of a community-centered approach to natural disasters.

2. *Build storytelling capability.* We are no longer surprised to be greeted by people with titles like "chief storyteller." But it remains the case that there is not enough investment in good narrative building in most organizations. It is difficult to motivate change in the face of a skeptical audience fed on a bland diet of facts and PowerPoint. The Nature Conservancy, for example, helps its 1,200 trustees hone their storytelling skills so they can develop strong narratives, engage audiences, and catalyze philanthropic giving.

3. *Practice reframing.* Arguments on climate change typically go like this: Proponents say we need major new commitments to limit temperature change below 2 degrees Celsius; opponents counter that this will lead to job losses and social disruption. It is a dialog where each side speaks past the other. We need new frames to change the static debate. A good example is a recent *Forbes* magazine article on the promise of transition from a coal-centered economy in Appalachia.[23] The article sets out the case for new tech jobs in renewable energy, how Appalachia can capitalize on its powerline infrastructure to export clean energy, and how the region is one of the top three most important ecosystems on the planet for carbon capture. It reframes the debate around the transformation of a local economy rather than the threat of job losses.

4. *Conspire with the CEO.* In risky show-and-tell situations in particular, it helps if the CEO is a co-conspirator, as we saw with the Federal Reserve case "Robbing the Bank." One show-and-tell idea in these days

of heightened cybersecurity might be to gain the attention of complacent colleagues through a staged cyberattack. Such an exercise could test defenses, expose weak links, and even include no-holds-barred feedback from a valued customer.

5. *Execute with surprise and novelty.* There is enormous value in using surprise and novelty to change hearts and minds. Today it's unusual when someone makes a presentation without PowerPoint, or when they bring just a single visual to a two-hour meeting rather than a sheaf of slides. In a presentation to board directors of a major philanthropic foundation the head of strategy captured the attention of her audience with a single diagram that showed on-ramps to social disadvantage from unemployment, incomplete education, and domestic violence (see Exhibit 6.9). Then she highlighted several off-ramps from social disadvantage, including job training programs and early childhood support to mothers—a simple but effective message.

ON AND OFF RAMPS TO SOCIAL DISADVANTAGE

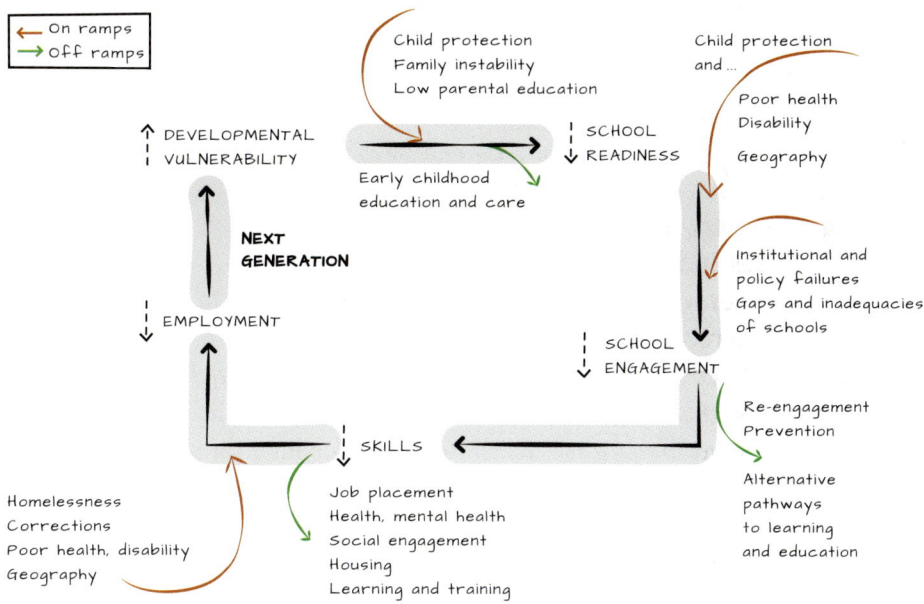

Exhibit 6.9

SOURCE: PAUL RAMSAY FOUNDATION, 2019.

Getting action to follow from problem solving has always been the acid test of our work. It feels a lot harder today—despite more data and visualization tools being available. Think of show and tell as a mindset that transforms you into a theater director creating a mini-production with props, *dramatis personae,* and a script. It's the final stage of problem solving with high uncertainty, but one now even more crucial to getting things done.

Chapter 7
Epilogue: All Strategies Are Wagers

Pascal's Wager

Sometime in the mid-1600s, the French philosopher Blaise Pascal was puzzling one of life's greatest conundrums: whether or not to believe in God. This wasn't idle speculation; it was existential. If God exists and Pascal didn't have faith, he would suffer the consequences of hell for eternity. He was in anguish. "If I saw no signs of a divinity," Pascal recorded, "I would fix myself in denial. If I saw everywhere the marks of a Creator, I would repose peacefully in faith. But seeing too much to deny Him, and too little to assure me, I am in a pitiful state, and I would wish a hundred times that if a god sustains nature it would reveal Him without ambiguity."[1]

Pascal viewed this decision like a bet—a wager on whether or not there is a divine being—with terrible consequences if the bet went wrong. From his perspective, it is a decision we are all forced to make, and one for which there is fundamental uncertainty. Before our deaths we cannot prove the existence of God. Like it or not, we must face the uncertainty and make a choice. The payoffs, moreover, are asymmetric: If you believe in God, and God doesn't really exist, your costs are modest—the time you have spent in church, and perhaps the money you put in the collection plate. But if you do not believe in God, and a vengeful God does exist, your costs are infinite, eternal damnation. This philosophical problem, which has come to be known as Pascal's wager, can be represented like Exhibit 7.1.

We don't know if this is good theology, but students of decision making, devout and irreverent, can avow that it was a cogent framing.[2] The structure of Pascal's wager helps us see important elements of any problem to be solved under uncertainty. It shows us that all strategies are wagers on an uncertain future; that it can be very difficult to assess the odds of each outcome in advance; that we have to take into account the costs of inaction, not just action; and, that there are hard cases where there is no chance to experiment and learn from small failures. Annie

PASCAL'S WAGER

State of Nature	Believe in God	Don't Believe in God
God Exists	Heaven	Hell
God Doesn't Exist	Cost of Attending Church	0

Exhibit 7.1

Duke, cognitive psychologist and former professional champion poker player, put it this way: "Our decisions are always bets. We routinely decide among alternatives, put resources at risk, assess the likelihood of different outcomes, and consider what it is that we value."[3]

The purpose of this short epilogue chapter is to provide a guide to understanding the nature of your strategy problem before you apply the mindsets that this book is about. This involves setting out your understanding of the structure of the problem, the stakes involved in moving forward, and the nature of the uncertainty you face. If you don't have a clear grasp of these elements, your problem solving can go horribly wrong. Pascal was able to represent his problem in a clear decision matrix—the goal of this chapter is to give you a similar clarity around the decisions you face. You can apply the lessons of the six mindsets without reading this chapter, but we think good preparation will give you better results.

Understand the Structure of the Problem

For all its gravity, Pascal's conundrum had a relatively simple structure: There is only one other player (God, who either exists or doesn't exist), one end state (death, which is irreversible), and two possible payoffs (heaven or hell). That means we can easily summarize Pascal's decision in a neat rubric that combines all three elements, as we saw earlier.

Not all problems are as easy to represent as the imponderables of eternity! But whenever you face a problem or decision, the best way to start is to understand its structure. Ideally you can draw that as a *game matrix* or *decision tree* to clarify the nature of your choices. As we saw in the Introduction 1, Nobel Laureate Herb Simon said that problem solving is "simply representing your problem so as to make the solution transparent". He guided us "to construct a simplified model of the real situation in order to deal with it."[4] We often find it useful to describe the elements of problem structure in the language of games: players, plays, timeframes, choices, and outcomes (see Exhibit 7.2). Let's look at these elements.

UNDERSTANDING PROBLEM STRUCTURE

Elements	Considerations
Other players	• How many? • Do their choices affect my outcomes?
Number of plays	• Multi-play games provide opportunities to learn, try different strategies, or even evolve competitive behavior
Reversibility and irreversibility	• Irreversibility raises the stakes and constrains learning opportunities
Binary or continuous choices	• Nonbinary choices and distributed outcomes provide scope for low cost learning and building cooperation • Winner-take-all games are tough!
Timeframes and set-plays	• More distant choices provide time to gather information on uncertainty • Short timeframes benefit from set-play planning

Exhibit 7.2

Other Players

In many types of problem, the choice does not depend on the behavior of other actors, at least in any obvious way. In this kind of problem, a decision tree is a useful way to visualize the structure of the problem. For example, if you are looking to buy an electric car (EV) instead of a conventional internal combustion engine car (ICE), you mainly care about the costs over your ownership period and the potential reduction in your carbon footprint. Subsidy and charging network policies could change and affect your decision, but they are largely knowable at the time of purchase. Let's look at a decision tree for a car buyer choosing between the Toyota Camry ICE and the Tesla Model 3 EV, a useful model for this kind of decision (see Exhibit 7.3). Is it a slam dunk for the EV?

ELECTRIC VEHICLE DECISION

(All $ present value (PV); carbon in metric tonnes (MT))

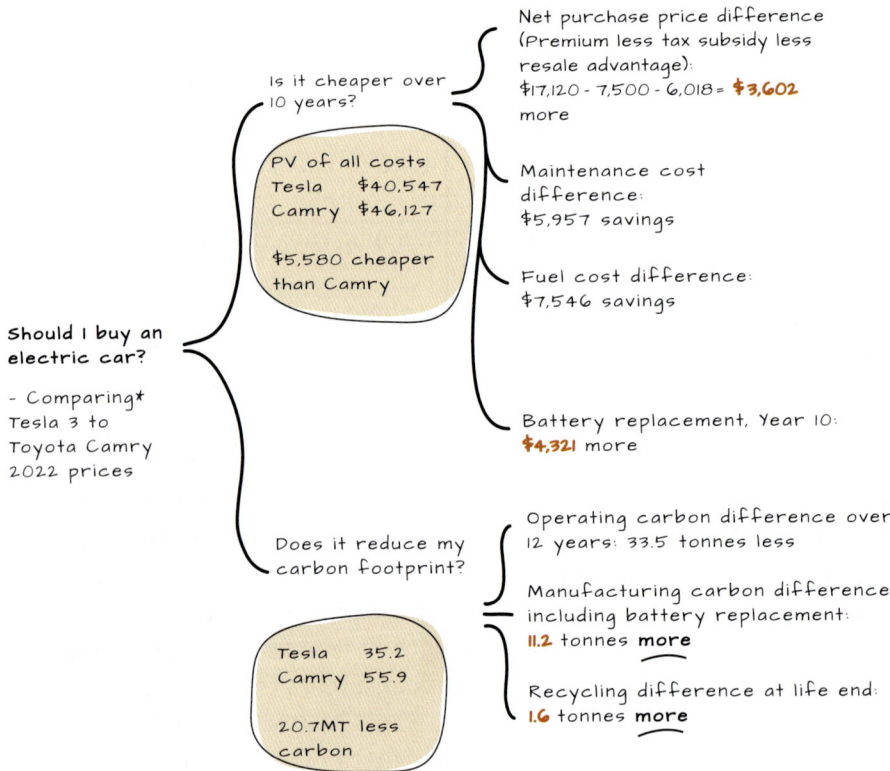

Is it cheaper over 10 years?

Net purchase price difference (Premium less tax subsidy less resale advantage): $17,120 - 7,500 - 6,018 = **$3,602** more

PV of all costs
Tesla $40,547
Camry $46,127

$5,580 cheaper than Camry

Maintenance cost difference: $5,957 savings

Fuel cost difference: $7,546 savings

Should I buy an electric car?

- Comparing*
Tesla 3 to
Toyota Camry
2022 prices

Battery replacement, Year 10: **$4,321** more

Does it reduce my carbon footprint?

Operating carbon difference over 12 years: 33.5 tonnes less

Manufacturing carbon difference; including battery replacement: **11.2 tonnes more**

Tesla   35.2
Camry   55.9

20.7MT less carbon

Recycling difference at life end: **1.6 tonnes more**

* Assumes: US case; 10,000 annual miles; grid uses 60% fossil fuel; 12 year ownership; battery replacement year 10

Exhibit 7.3

The EV cost $17,000 more at the day of purchase in 2022, but with the current tax credit and lower operating costs, the total present value of cost of ownership over 10 years for a US car purchaser is around $5,580 less for the Tesla. Not a big difference really, especially as EV prices have been increasing faster than ICE prices in 2022—and one that is very dependent on the tax subsidy.

But does the EV reduce a car buyer's carbon footprint over the ICE? You would think this is an easy one, but it's not that simple. Yes, the electric grid in the United States—which uses roughly 40% non-fossil-fuel sources—gives the EV an operating carbon advantage over gasoline. But this is partly offset by the carbon emissions from manufacturing and end-of-life recycling, especially if you replace the battery in year 10. The net advantage to the EV is only 20.7 tonnes over 12 years—not much, considering the typical American is responsible for approximately 20 metric tonnes annually. So, there is some advantage of the EV over the ICE, but it isn't very large in terms of costs or avoided carbon.

In this kind of situation, where the problem revolves around a single actor (you), a decision tree provides a good visualization of the problem structure and solution. It also highlights sensitivity to relatively small changes in assumptions (electric grid fuel mix, subsidy level, battery replacement, miles driven).

With other problems, the moves or choices of other actors are central to the structure of decisions. In many games, such as chess, each move by an opponent changes the choices and odds you face on your subsequent move. The same goes for many business decisions, where outcomes are affected by the strategic moves (pricing, new products, new market entry) of competitors. In 2011, for example, Israeli food company Tnuva determined that local demand for cottage cheese would support a 15% price hike (we are told that if there is one thing that people in Israel can agree on, it is that they all love cottage cheese). Raising the price of cottage cheese just as Facebook was coming into its own, however, allowed small groups of consumers to organize online, leading to massive protests and a committed boycott. Soon the government launched an investigation of the higher prices—and finally imposed price controls that resulted in *lowering* the price of cottage cheese by 20%. Tnuva should have thought more about the reaction of other actors to its pricing strategy.

Number of Plays

If there is a single decision point for your problem, there is no opportunity to learn, to try different strategies, or to influence the behavior of other actors. If there are many plays, there is a chance to learn more about the characteristics of the game and other actors' behavior, and therefore to develop better strategies along the way.

You are no doubt familiar with the Prisoner's Dilemma, a game in which two petty criminals are interrogated separately about a crime they committed together. Each faces a problem: Do I stay silent, hoping my colleague stays silent too, in which case we both serve only one year in jail; or, do I betray my colleague, who then serves three years if he stayed silent, while I have the chance to go free? The catch is that if both prisoners betray each other, both serve two years, a total of four years served (see Exhibit 7.4). The best outcome would be for both players to keep

PRISONER'S DILEMMA

		PRISONER A	
		Stays silent (Co-operates)	Betrays B (Defects)
PRISONER B	Stays silent	Both serve 1 year	A goes free B gets 3 years
	Betrays A	B goes free A gets 3 years	Both serve 2 years

Exhibit 7.4

quiet (serving only two years in total)—but the temptation to betray the other and go free is too strong, and the outcome is always that both cheat, betray the other, and get the worst combined outcome. In a single-play game with no chance to send a signal to each other, the bad outcome is nearly inevitable.

In an interesting twist, political scientist Robert Axelrod has shown in both computer simulations and real-world tournaments that playing the Prisoner's Dilemma many times, with an uncertain ending point, encourages cooperation between the players. They can actually move toward the better joint outcome by staying mutually silent. How do they do that? In this case, the best problem solving is a strategy called tit-for-tat: Never betray first and mimic the move of your opponent on the next play of the game—reward cooperation and punish defection. Notice that it introduces a kind of forgiveness: If your opponent cooperates on a play (stays silent), you reward this behavior by mimicking it, even if that opponent hurt you previously.

Problems with a structure like the Prisoner's Dilemma are common in business. Think of price wars that break out between adjacent gas stations, or between supermarkets over the price of milk, or airlines flying popular routes, or banks setting consumer interest rates. If there is a single play and no way to learn, the individual players always do the thing that is best only for themselves, ensuring a bad outcome for all. If there are multiple plays, it may be that both learn to cooperate, which in these cases is good for the companies but bad for consumers!

This strategy is entirely consistent with our idea of imperfectionism as a key mindset for problem solving: Step into risk with small moves that reveal information about the structure of the problem, get a sense of probabilities, gauge the behavior of other actors, and build knowledge to make bigger bets.

Reversibility and Irreversibility

Sometimes decisions are reversible. You can try an approach, assess the outcome, and, if you don't like it, reverse the original choice. If the costs are low enough, it is worth paying the price to learn. Amazon founder Jeff Bezos separates the company's strategic moves into irreversible and reversible decisions, and emphasizes how important it is to be able to decide quickly in the case of the latter. Amazon prefers to err on the side of moving boldly, learning from small-consequence decisions. In his 2015 Letter to Shareholders, Bezos explained,

> *"Some decisions are consequential and irreversible or nearly irreversible— one-way doors—and these decisions must be made methodically, carefully, slowly, with great deliberation and consultation . . . But most decisions aren't like that—they are changeable, reversible . . . you don't have to live with the consequences for that long . . . [These] decisions can and should be made quickly by high judgment individuals or small groups. As organizations get larger, there seems to be a tendency to use the heavy- weight . . . decision-making process on most decisions . . . The end result of this is slowness, unthoughtful risk aversion, failure to experiment suffi- ciently, and consequently diminished invention".*[5]

But can large corporations, particularly from traditional industries, really make major decisions this way? Yes. A good example of a reversible decision was the ill-fated launch of New Coke in 1985, purportedly in response to blind taste tests that favored Pepsi. The Coca-Cola company hadn't changed its secret recipe since the first glass of Coke was served in 1886—a period of 99 years! However, slowly eroding market share and blind tastings finally convinced executives to follow this risky route. The decision provoked outrage among consumers, who flooded the company's complaint telephone line. CEO Roberto Goizueta received one angry letter addressed to "Chief Dodo, The Coca-Cola Company." (He later joked that he was upset because the office knew to deliver it to him.)[6] Only 79 days after the launch, Coca-Cola reintroduced the original Coke as Coke Classic. It downplayed New Coke, and finally withdrew it entirely in 2002. Notwithstanding the short-term costs of failure, the decision proved to be a marketing boon and a sales boost for Coke Classic—and a way to build greater knowledge about its customers. Most important, the decision was reversible.

Binary or Continuous

Another way of thinking about the nature of your decision is to identify whether the choices and outcomes are binary or continuous. If you can try a *little* of a particular approach—a small experiment with low costs—you can learn from small wins or losses and improve your strategy. You can also demonstrate intent to competitors and perhaps build cooperative outcomes. Binary choices, single-play games, and winner-take-all outcomes, on the other hand, don't foster iterative learning or collaboration. These are the ones to be really careful with.

Timeframes and Set-Plays

Short timeframes, especially with irreversible choices and binary outcomes, put pressure on problem solvers. When we're under stress, it's human nature to fall back on conventional and conservative answers. Great problem solving organizations seek to counter this tendency by developing *set-plays*. We borrow the idea of set-plays from sports and theater. In sports, people practice games by setting up difficult problem solving situations that they could face in the future. They then play that game out in advance, on paper and on the practice field, to develop alternative strategies. Think about corner kicks or penalty kicks in soccer; teams practice set-plays that they believe will get through defenses and score. Take the "Panenka kick" used by penalty takers, when a player daringly chips the ball lightly to the center of the goal, gambling that the goalkeeper will dive hard to the left or to the right. The play is named after the Czech soccer player Antonín Panenka, who stunned the powerful West German team with his carefully rehearsed maneuver. Some teams even have set-play coaches.

Many organizations test their strategic options in a similar way, using a red team/blue team or "war games" approach. One side makes the case for the strategic option ("here's how it will lead to a great outcome") and the other side's job is to attack the strategy and poke holes in it. The WL Gore company even gives a prize to those who are best at pointing out faults, the *sharpshooter* award.[7]

Good problem solving organizations employ a related technique, the *pre-mortem*. They imagine in detail how a particular decision they are about to take would play out if it failed to work. In this way key actors can consider in advance what they can do to mitigate the risks and forestall bad outcomes. Both of these ideas are forms of thought experiment, ways to prepare for the time pressures of game day.

Weigh the Stakes

Problem solving is a wager on the future, so we need to understand the stakes, or costs, of playing the game. That means assessing the costs of each strategic move—including the costs of doing nothing—and weighing the payoffs of each potential outcome. Seasoned problem solvers take great care to avoid "wish-casting": They honestly weigh their resources and capabilities relative to the cost to play—and perhaps lose. Those with deep pockets or the ability to borrow can be bolder. Those with tight finances are better off entertaining lower-consequence strategic moves.

Remember that there are many types of bias in our human decision making. Decision makers who are overconfident underestimate the costs of being wrong and overstate the benefits of being right. They are often also prone to availability bias, anchoring their mind in a positive experience that colors their thinking about the new problem. Nicholas Taleb has written about this kind of mistake in investing businesses.[8] Financial traders who buy an asset that then rises in price tend to "backward fit" a theory or model to explain why the asset went up—often, one that is entirely wrong. They then employ this model on their next trade, confidently believing they have found the secret to beating the market. Usually they haven't.

As we have seen, the flipside of the overconfidence bias, risk aversion, is a bigger danger for most organizations.[9] Managers spend a lot of time and energy documenting and assessing the cost of errors of *commission*—that is, bad outcomes as a result of doing something. The risk committee of every major company carefully evaluates all the things that could go wrong and develops plans to limit these risks. That is sensible, of course, but these same committees nearly always fail to assess the costs of inaction, the risk of *omission*.

These two types of risk-taking mistakes are often called Type 1 errors (committing a mistake) and Type 2 errors (missing or omitting an opportunity). Successful incumbent companies often make both types of mistake in the face of new entrant risk. Think of the newspaper industry's reaction to the fledgling steps of new internet players in the mid-1990s, which we looked at in the Introduction. Incumbent newspaper company managers massively underestimated the probabilities of success of these new challengers, and of the impact on their own business. They pointed to their hundreds of years of experience of producing great content and dominating local advertising markets. This was a real and substantial advantage, of course. But they failed to see the dual threats of user-created content and newer and better ways to market cars, houses, and jobs online. They didn't see that the attack would come from *behind*, destroying the powerful engine of newspaper profitability, display and classified advertising. Newspaper companies didn't understand the stakes of the game they found themselves playing, or the odds.

Estimate the Odds

The third element to get right in understanding your problem is to know the nature and level of the risk you face, in order to get a sense of the odds of each move. Academics have long distinguished between risk, which is uncertainty where probabilities can be established, and true uncertainty or ambiguity, where probabilities cannot be estimated (sometimes called Knightian uncertainty, after Frank Knight). Economists John Kay and Mervyn King call this *radical uncertainty*, where in contrast to physical laws or probabilistic games, uncertainty cannot be adequately described or resolved. In those circumstances, they argue that "conventional statistical inference rarely applies and forecasts are often based on shifting sands."[10]

The real world we live in has many types of uncertainty; reality unfolds as the complex interplay of stochastic events and human reactions. We typically don't face situations at work with simple, knowable odds, like a roulette table. COVID-19 is an obvious example: Humanity dealt with the health and economic effects of the disease, and their complex interactions, with relatively little recent prior knowledge and only a limited sense of probabilities.

Presidential Imperfectionists

Former US president Harry Truman put a sign on his desk: "The buck stops here." The message was that decisions were not to be avoided—other people had "passed the buck," and now this president was going to decide. But would those decisions lead to good outcomes? More than 60 years later, President Barack Obama explained that "no problem that landed on my desk, foreign or domestic, had a clean, 100 percent solution. If it had, someone else down the chain of command would have solved it already. Instead, I was constantly dealing with probabilities: a 70 percent chance, say, that a decision to do nothing would end in disaster; a 55 percent chance that this approach versus one that might solve the problem (with a zero percent chance that it would work out exactly as intended); a 30 percent chance that whatever we chose wouldn't work at all, along with a 15 percent chance that it would make the problem worse. In such circumstances, chasing after the perfect solution led to paralysis."[12]

Guesses based on gut instinct can go wildly wrong. That's why one of the keys to operating in uncertain environments is "epistemic humility," which Eric Angner defines as ". . . the realization that our knowledge is always provisional and incomplete—and that it might require revision in light of new evidence."[11] How to seek out new data to modify your views, a topic we covered in the occurrent behavior mindset, is vital to being a good problem solver under uncertainty.

There is no one-size-fits-all approach to determining the nature of uncertainty, but we have found this simple framework, developed by some former colleagues, to be useful (see Exhibit 7.5).[13] It separates uncertainty into five levels, beginning with known unknowns—that is, where you understand the sources of uncertainty and can make reasonable predictions of the odds. A good example of this level of uncertainty would be projecting next year's mobile phone sales.

WHAT IS THE LEVEL OF UNCERTAINTY?

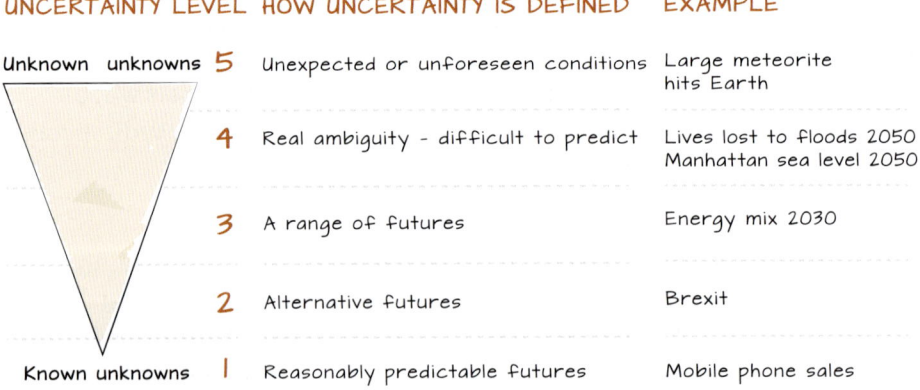

UNCERTAINTY LEVEL		HOW UNCERTAINTY IS DEFINED	EXAMPLE
Unknown unknowns	5	Unexpected or unforeseen conditions	Large meteorite hits Earth
	4	Real ambiguity - difficult to predict	Lives lost to floods 2050 Manhattan sea level 2050
	3	A range of futures	Energy mix 2030
	2	Alternative futures	Brexit
Known unknowns	1	Reasonably predictable futures	Mobile phone sales

Exhibit 7.5
SOURCE: HUGH COURTNEY, MCKINSEY QUARTERLY.

Level 2 uncertainty is where there are alternative futures created, say, by a shift in government policy or the introduction of a new technology. We can understand the elements of uncertainty, and make reasonable guesses about binary outcomes. A good example is the nature of uncertainty about the Brexit policy change in the UK. Level 3 uncertainty describes a broader range of future states when it isn't clear which is more likely and what the outcomes for key variables would be, for example the mix of worldwide energy use 10 years from now. This is where probability assessment begins to get hard.

Level 4 uncertainty is real ambiguity, when it becomes challenging but not impossible to characterize the range of future states and the nature of systems that could prevail in them. Here one might include sea levels in 2050, which are subject to many complex and interrelated factors, or the percentage of Antarctica remaining intact that same year. Finally, level 5 uncertainty is the world of unknown unknowns, the kind of uncertainty where we cannot even conceive of all the variables at play in future states. As a boy John Pershing witnessed a skirmish in the American Civil War known as "bushwacking"—a type of guerrilla attack. But the young Pershing, who would become America's commanding general in Europe during World War I, could at the time never have imagined another type of warfare he would live to see decades later in the 1940s, nuclear mutually assured destruction.

When you face problems with level 1 or 2 uncertainty you can make educated guesses about potential outcomes and their likelihood. If you have good capabilities, resources, and time, in these circumstances you can make bolder wagers. In situations of level 3 or 4 uncertainty—or where you are short on capabilities and resources—better approaches will be smaller moves where you edge into risk and build knowledge and capability. We talked about this in the Imperfectionism chapter.

* * *

All real-life strategic problem solving is a wager on an uncertain world. Fortified with a good understanding of your problem's structure, stakes, and odds, and armed with the six mindsets, we hope you are well equipped to overcome risk aversion and confidently step into uncertainty as a full-fledged imperfectionist.

Appendix: Bulletproof Problem Solving

A Disciplined Toolset for Great Problem Solving

In *Bulletproof Problem Solving: The One Skill That Changes Everything* (Wiley 2019), we provide a toolset for disciplined problem solving. The appeal of the approach is that the same systematic process can be used to solve almost every kind of problem, from simple ones to those with complex interdependencies. It sets out a simple but rigorous approach to defining problems, disaggregating them into manageable pieces, focusing good analytic tools on the most important parts, and then synthesizing findings to tell a powerful story. This toolset dovetails nicely with the problem solving mindsets described in this volume.

Step 1: Define the Problem. Getting a crystal-clear definition of the problem you are solving is the critical starting point to bulletproof problem solving. And it should be relatively straightforward. But a surprising number of failures in problem solving originate in poor problem definition. Teams and individuals surge off into data gathering or expert interviews without being very clear about the boundaries of the problem, the criteria for success, the timeframe, or the level of accuracy required.

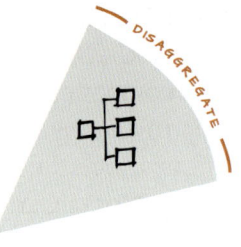

Step 2: Disaggregate the Problem. Any problem of real consequence is too complicated to solve without breaking it down into logical parts that help us understand the *drivers or causes* of the situation. We use cleaving frames to test different logic tree structures to see which provides the greatest insight into solution paths. The magic comes in seeing which type of logic tree makes an elegant solution more obvious.

Step 3: Prioritize the Issues. Good problem solving is just as much about what you don't do as what you do, and good prioritization in problem solving makes solutions come faster and with less effort. We want our initial trees to be mutually exclusive and collectively exhaustive, so that we know we have all the parts. But we don't want to retain elements of the disaggregation that have only a small influence on the problem, or that are difficult or impossible to affect. Before we start to invest significant time and effort into work planning and analysis, we have to prune our trees.

Step 4: Build a Workplan and Timetable. Once the problem's component parts are disaggregated and prioritized, you then link each part to a plan for fact gathering and analysis. This plan assigns team members to each analytic task with specific outputs and completion dates. A good work-planning process also includes team norms around generating a diversity of views, role playing, and flattening hierarchy to avoid biases and achieve better answers. Great one-day answers drive speed.

Step 5: Conduct critical analyses. We start with simple heuristics and summary statistics to get a clear picture of each problem component. This helps us understand when to employ more complex analytic techniques, including multiple regression, game theory, Monte Carlo simulation, and machine learning. Which of the analytic big guns to deploy depends on whether we need to know the value of a driver or predict an outcome, and on whether the answer can be affected by the behavior of other actors.

Steps 6 and 7: Synthesize & Communicate. Great problem solving motivates decision makers to act. Analytic findings must be synthesized into arguments with supporting data. Then a powerful storyline is developed around the governing idea for change, and that links back to the original problem statement, including the decision maker's criteria for success, boundaries, and need for precision. To be compelling, the storyline needs to be supported by logic, analysis, and data, and speak the decision maker's values. Several argument structures may be employed according to the situation.

Although we describe the seven steps in a linear fashion, it is best thought of as an iterative process that you loop through each day ("What is my best guess today?"), each week with your team, and over the course of the time you have to solve your problem. Done well, it is a disciplined approach that can crack almost every problem with creativity.

Notes

Introduction: Becoming an Imperfectionist

1. L. Muehlhauser, "Three Wild Speculations From Amateur Quantitative Macrohistory," Blog post, September 12, 2017, accessed at https://Lukemuehlhauser.Com/Three-Wild-Speculations-From-Amateur-Quantitative-Macrohistory/.
2. "Zero to $12bn: Tiktok Is Hitting Revenue Milestones Very Quickly," Chartr, June 29, 2022, accessed at https://www.chartr.co/stories/2022-06-29-2-tiktok-is-hitting-milestones-quickly.

Chapter 1 Ever Curious

1. "The Idea of Instant Photography," Baker Library Historical Collections, Harvard Business School.
2. Private communication with Professor Barry Marshall.
3. George Loewenstein, "The Psychology of Curiosity: A Review and Reinterpretation," *Psychological Bulletin* 116, no. 1 (1994): 75.
4. A. S. Honig, S. A. Miller, and E. B. Church, "Ages and Stages: How Curiosity Leads to Learning," *Early Childhood Today*, October 2006.
5. C. Kidd and B. Y. Hayden, "The Psychology and Neuroscience of Curiosity," *Neuron* 88, no. 3 (November 4, 2015): 449–460.
6. Ibid.
7. B. D. Perry, "Why Young Children Are Curious," *Early Childhood Today* 17, no. 4 (2003): 26–27.
8. S. Grimes, "Walt Disney on Curiosity," *The 1000 Day MFA*, March 5, 2019. https://medium.com/the-1000-day-mfa/walt-disney-on-curiosity-215ab2769d0d.
9. F. Gino, "The Business Case for Curiosity," *Harvard Business Review*, September–October 2018.
10. J. D'Onfro, "The Truth About Google's Famous 20% Time Policy," *Business Insider*, April 17, 2015.
11. M. Violaris, "Einstein at the Patent Office," *The Oxford Scientist*, Michaelmas term issue, 2019.
12. P. Galison, "Einstein's Clocks: The Place of Time," *Critical Inquiry* 26, no. 2 (Winter 2000): 367.

13. Ibid., 377.

14. Ibid.

15. A. Boutsko, "New Bach Discovery Raises Questions of Burnout," *DW*, December 27, 2013, https://www.dw.com/en/new-bach-discovery-raises-question-of-burn-out/a-17326653.

16. D. Herscovitch, "Decoding the Music Masterpieces: Bach's *Art of Fugue*," *The Conversation*, March 23, 2017, https://theconversation.com/decoding-the-music-masterpieces-bachs-the-art-of-fugue-73522.

17. "Did Bach Really Leave *Art of Fugue* Unfinished?" Pipedreams, American Public Media, 2022, https://pipedreams.publicradio.org/articles/artoffugue/unfinished.shtml.

18. R. Flanagan, *The Narrow Road to the Deep North* (New York: Vintage Books, 2013).

19. C. Sullivan, "Nasal Positive Airway Pressure and Sleep Apnea," *American Journal of Respiratory Critical Care Medicine* 198, no 5 (September 1, 2018): 581–587. Also: Personal communication with Peter Farrell, January 6, 2022.

20. Ibid., 581.

21. A. Vance, *Elon Musk: How the Billionaire CEO of Space X and Tesla Is Shaping Our Future* (London: Virgin Books, 2016).

22. Personal communication with Eric Schmidt, March 10, 2022.

23. Personal communication with Professor Robert Wood, May 2022.

24. D. Hamilton, *Cracking the Curiosity Code* (Columbus: Gatekeeper Press, 2019).

Chapter 2 Dragonfly Eye

1. A. L. Oppenheim, *Ancient Mesopotamia: Portrait of a Dead Civilization*, revised edition (Chicago: University of Chicago Press, 1977).

2. Personal communication with Ronald Cohen.

3. Ibid.

4. E. Disley, Chris Giacomantonio, Kristy Kruithof, and Megan Sim, "The Payment by Results Social Impact Bond Pilot at HMP Peterborough: Final Process Evaluation Report," RAND Europe, February 6, 2016.

5. Personal communication with Sir Ronald Cohen, 2021.

6. P. E. Tetlock and D. Gardner, *Superforecasting: The Art and Science of Prediction* (New York: Random House, 2015), 124.

7. Ford Motor Company, "Ford Accelerating Transformation: Forming Distinct Auto Units to Scale EVs, Strengthen Operations, Unlock Value," Presentation, March 2, 2022.

8. E. de Bono, *Six Thinking Hats* (New York: Viking, 1986), 45.

9. Personal communication with Chris Bradley, November 30, 2021.

10. Personal communication with Konvoy founder Adam Trippe-Smith, March 22, 2022.

11. R. Forshaw, "Orthodontics in Antiquity: Myth or Reality," *British Dental Journal* 221 (2016): 137–140.

12. Personal communication with Kelsey Wirth.

13. http://peterfisk.com, February 17, 2020.

14. K. Booker, "WeFail: How the Doomed Masa Son–Adam Neumann Relationship Set WeWork on the Road to Disaster," *Fast Company*, November 15, 2019.

15. The We Company SEC S1. Accessed August 24, 2019. https://www.sec.gov/Archives/edgar/data/1533523/000119312519220499/d781982ds1.htm.

16. H. Ford, *My Life and Work* (New York: Doubleday, 1922).

17. G. Grandin, *Fordlandia: The Rise and Fall of Henry Ford's Forgotten Jungle City* (New York: Metropolitan Books, 2009). For what it's worth, Henry Ford II also insisted on driving only black cars. D. Halberstam, *The Reckoning* (New York: Avon Books, 1986).

18. A. Selipsky, Bloomberg Television, November 2, 2021.

19. R. Miller, "How AWS Came to Be," *TechCrunch*, July 2, 2016, https://guce.techcrunch.com/copyConsent?sessionId=3_cc-session_3c7ba777-d136-4581-9182-96e4322e7259&lang=en-US.

20. Ibid.

21. Harvard Innovation Labs, "Fireside Chat with Michael Skok and Andy Jassy: The History of Amazon Web Services," 2013. Retrieved from http://youtube/d2dyGDqrXL0.

22. "UW CSE Distinguished Lecture: Andy Jassy (AWS)," Paul Allen School [Video], 2017. Retrieved from http://www.youtube.com.watch?v=QVUqyOuNUB8&t=244s&ab-channnel=PaulGAllenSChool.

23. B. Black, "EC2 Origins" (blog post), January 25, 2009, https://blog.b3k.us/2009/01/25/ec2-origins.html.

24. N. Cubrilovic, "Almost Exclusive: Amazon Readies Utility Computing Service," *TechCrunch*, August 24, 2006. https://techcrunch.com/2006/08/24/exclusive-amazon-readies-utility-computing-service/.

25. Gartner, Market Share: IT Services, Worldwide 2020 [Dataset]/Global market share data for 2020, https://www.gartner.com/en/documents/4000294.

26. A. Alexander, *A Stranger Truth: Lessons in Love, Leadership and Courage from India's Sex Workers* (New Delhi: Juggernaut Publications, 2018).

27. D. Barton and G. Kumra, "Leading in the 21st Century," McKinsey & Company, December 4, 2013, www.mckinsey.com/business-functions/strategy-and-corporate-finance/our-insights/leading-in-the-21st-century.

28. S. Parrish, *The Great Mental Models*, vol. 1 (Ottawa: Latticework Publishing, 2019).

29. Personal communication with Lawrence Fung, February 21, 2022.

30. I. Gerretsen, "The Remarkable Power of Australian Kelp," BBC Future Planet, April 14, 2021. https://www.bbc.com>future>article>20210406).

31. Interview with Aiden Soedjarwo, November 15, 2021.

32. J. McGlashan, J. Hayward, A. Brown, B. Owen, L. Millar, M. Johnstone, D. Creighton, and S. Allendar, "Comparing Complex Perspectives on Obesity Drivers: Action-Driven Communities and Evidence-Oriented Experts," *Obesity Science and Practice* 4, no. 6 (November 22, 2018): 575–581. doi: 10.1002/osp4.306. PMID: 30574350; PMCID: PMC6298210.

33. See, e.g., R. Dobbs, C. Sawers, F. Thompson, J. Manyika, J. Woetzel, P. Child, S. McKenna, and A. Spatharou, *Overcoming Obesity: An Initial Economic Analysis* (McKinsey Global Institute, November 2014).

Chapter 3 Occurrent Behavior

1. Personal conversation with Ted Hall and Don Watters.

2. H. A. Simon, *The Sciences of the Artificial* (Cambridge, MA: MIT Press, 1969).

3. S. Samuel, "When a California City Gave People a Guaranteed Income, They Worked More—Not Less," *Vox*, March 6, 2021.

4. B. Wodecki, "Human Error Causes 99% of Autonomous Vehicle Accidents: Study," *IoT World Today*, October 20, 2021.

5. H. Jones, "The Recent Large Reduction in Space Launch Cost," 48th International Conference on Environmental Systems, ICES-81, (1), 2018.

6. IDEO U, *Innovation in Orbit: Insights from NASA and Space X interview with Garrett Reisman*, podcast, 2020.

7. M. Sheetz, "Space X Caught the Nose Cone of Its Falcon Heavy Rocket for the First Time in the Net of a Boat," CNBC Online, June 25, 2019, https://www.cnbc.com/2019/06/25/spacex-caught-falcon-heavy-rocket-nose-cone-in-net-of-high-speed-boat.html.

8. W. Cobb, "How Space X Lowered Costs and Reduced Barriers to Space," *The Conversation*, March 1, 2019, http://www.theconversation.com.

9. H. Jones, "The Recent Large Reduction In Space Launch Cost," paper presented at the 48th International Conference on Environmental Systems, National Aeronautics and Space Administration, Albuquerque, NM, 2018.

10. Personal communication with Alex Burke, CEO, Education Perfect.

11. "Factbox: How Do Ride-Hailing Giants Didi and Uber Compare?" *Reuters*, July 1, 2021.

12. J. Crabtree, "Didi Chuxing Took on Uber and Won. Now It's Taking on the World," *Wired*, September 2, 2018, https://www.wired.co.uk/article/didi-chuxing-china-startups-uber.

13. M. Smith, "She Built China's Uber. She's Coming for Australia," *Financial Review*, September 13, 2019, https://www.afr.com/world/asia/she-built-china-s-uber-she-s-coming-for-australia-20190808-p52f9e.

14. J. Liu and D. Rubenstein, *The David Rubenstein Show*: Didi President Jean Liu, Bloomberg Insights [TV], New York.

15. C. Shepherd "Jean Liu Drives Didi's International Image," *Financial Times*, July 2, 2021, https://www.ft.com/content/ad10ab97-40dc-4c2a-b621-bfc675601b33.

16. Smith, "She Built China's Uber."

17. Liu, and Rubenstein, *The David Rubenstein Show*.

18. Crabtree, "Didi Chuxing Took on Uber and Won."

19. Liu and Rubenstein, *The David Rubenstein Show*.

20. Smith, "She Built China's Uber."

21. Crabtree, "Didi Chuxing Took on Uber and Won."

22. U. Shamir and C. D. D. Howard, "An Analytic Approach to Scheduling Pipe Replacement," *Journal AWWA*, May 1, 1979, https://awwa.onlinelibrary.wiley.com/doi/epdf/10.1002/j.1551-8833.1979.tb04345.x?saml_referrer.

23. D. McCallum, "Advanced Pipe Sensing to Reduce Leaks and Breaks: Final Report," NSW Smart Sensing Network, December 2020, https://static1.squarespace.com/static/5b623bcfda02bce646ae3f10/t/60753c149142e268f0acf321/1618295868172/NSSN+Advanced+Pipe+Sensing+Final+Report+-+Apr21.pdf.

24. J. Askim and T. Bergström, "Between Lockdown and Calm Down. Comparing the COVID-19 Responses of Norway and Sweden," *Local Government Studies* 48, no. 2 (2022): 291–311.

25. Based on Askim and Bergstrom, ibid.

26. H. Wang et al., "Estimating Excess Mortality Due to the COVID-19 Pandemic: A Systematic Analysis of COVID-19-Related Mortality, 2020–21. *The Lancet*, March 10, 2022. Epidemiologists prefer the use of calculated excess deaths relative to historical averages, as compared to simple death rates, as there are often differences in death attribution when there are multiple causes, and because policies that lead to deaths due to some causes may be partly balanced by fewer deaths from other causes (for example, fewer highway deaths during lockdowns).

27. OECD *Country Economic Snapshot*, June 2022, https://www.oecd.org/about/secretary-general/oecd-secretary-general-mathias-cormann-launched-the-2022-oecd-economic-outlook-8-june-2022.htm.

28. S. Kessler, "Wendy's Is Responding to the Rising Minimum Wage by Replacing Humans with Robots," *Quartz*, March 3, 2017 (updated July 22, 2022), https://qz.com/923442/wendys-is-responding-to-the-rising-minimum-wage-by-replacing-humans-with-robots/.

29. D. Card and A. Krueger, "Minimum Wages and Employment: A Case Study of the Fast-Food Industry in New Jersey and Pennsylvania," *American Economic Review* 84, no. 4 (1994).

30. O. Ashenfelter, "Predicting the Quality and Prices of Bordeaux Wines," *The Economic Journal* 118 (2008): 174–184.

31. Ibid.

32. J. Marland, "How Big Data Can Predict the Wine of the Century," *Forbes*, April 30, 2014.

33. E. de Boer, "Avoid Pilot Purgatory in 7 Steps," *McKinsey Organization Blog*, April 16, 2018.

34. J. A. List, *The Voltage Effect* (New York: Penguin, 2022).

Chapter 4 Collective Intelligence

1. D. Sobel, *Longitude* (New York: Harper Perennial, 2008).

2. Ibid., 74.

3. P. E. Tetlock and D. Gardner, *Superforecasting: The Art and Science of Prediction* (New York: Crown Publishers/Random House, 2015).

4. T.-C. Pham, C.-M. Luong, V.-D. Hoang, and A. Doucet, "AI Outperformed Every Dermatologist in Dermoscopic Melanoma Diagnosis," *Nature* 11, no. 1 (September 1, 2021): 17485.

5. K. Boudreau, N. Lacetera, and K. Lakhani, "Incentives and Problem Uncertainty in Innovation Contests.," *Management Science* 57, no. 5 (2011): 843–863.

6. "Joy's law," Wikipedia, http://en.wikipedia.org, accessed August 10, 2022.

7. "Charles Lindbergh," Wikipedia, http://en.wikipedia.org.

8. FAO State of World Fisheries and Aquaculture, 2020, https://www.fao.org/documents/card/en/c/ca9229en/.

9. The Nature Conservancy, Ocean Stories: "FishFace," http://natureaustralia.org.au-what-we-do/our-priorities/oceans/ocean-stories/fishface/, accessed August 12, 2022.

10. GitHub, http://github.com, accessed February 21, 2022.

11. Private communication with Mark Zimring of The Nature Conservancy, January 2022.

12. Personal communication with Jordan Hubbard, September 2021.

13. Ibid.

14. Apache Foundation, http://www.apache.org, accessed August 12, 2022.

15. Microsoft, "Microsoft to Acquire GitHub for $7.5 Billion," press release, June 4, 2018, https://news.microsoft.com/2018/06/04/microsoft-to-acquire-github-for-7-5-billion/.

16. *Homebrew Computer Club Newsletter* 2, no. 1 (January 31, 1976).

17. Personal communication with Otto Campion, August 2021.

18. G. Mulgan, *Big Mind: How Collective Intelligence Can Change Our World* (Princeton, NJ: Princeton University Press, 2018).

19. G. Gigerenzer, *How to Stay Smart in a Smart World: Why Human Intelligence Still Beats Algorithms* (New York: Random House, 2022).

20. C. Stadler, "3 Lessons Startups Can Learn from Quibi's Failure," *Forbes*, November 24, 2020, http://www.forbes.com.

21. J. Katzenberg, and M. Whitman, "An open letter to the employees, investors, and partners who believed in Quibi and made this business possible," *Medium*, October 21, 2020, https://quibi-hq.medium.com/an-open-letter-from-quibi-8af6b415377f.

22. Stadler, "3 Lessons Startups Can Learn."

23. L. Rosenberg, N. Pescettelli, and G. Willcox, G. (2018). "Artificial Swarm Intelligence vs Vegas Betting Markets," IEEE, September 1, 2018.

24. The AlphaCode Team, "Competitive programming with AlphaCode," *Deep Mind* (blog), February 2, 2022, https://www.deepmind.com>blog>competitive-programming-with-alpha-code.

25. S. Vesuvala and S. Brown, "AI and Machine-Learning Tools Can Enhance Strategic Planning," McKinsey & Company, *Strategy and Corporate Finance Podcast*, November 23, 2021, https://www.mckinsey.com/capabilities/strategy-and-corporate-finance/our-insights/improving-strategic-outcomes-with-advanced-analytics.

26. Personal communication with Sasha Vesuvala.

27. T. Rose, *Collective Illusions: Conformity, Complicity and the Science of Why We Make Bad Decisions* (New York: Hachette Books, 2022).

Chapter 5 Imperfectionism

1. C. M. Christensen, R. Alton, C. Rising, and A. Waldeck, "The Big Idea: The New M&A Playbook," *Harvard Business Review*, March 2011. Of course, not all mergers fail. Bets can be bold *and* measured like Morgan Stanley's acquisition of Eaton

Vance and E*Trade in the middle of the Covid pandemic in 2020. These two acquisitions totaled $20 billion, slightly more than 15% of year-end market capitalization, and added critical assets and capability to the parent.

2. Barry Nalebuff reminds us that boxer Joe Lewis is credited with an earlier version of the same notion: B. Nalebuff, *Split the Pie: A Radical New Way to Negotiate* (New York: Harper, 2022).

3. D. Kahneman and A. Tversky, "Prospect Theory: An Analysis of Decision Under Risk," *Econometrica* 47, no. 2 (1979): 263–292.

4. D. Lovallo, T. Koller, R. Uhlanerand D. Kahneman, "Your Company Is Too Risk-Averse," *Harvard Business Review*, March–April 2020.

5. T. Koller, D. Lovallo, and Z. Williams, "Overcoming a Bias Against Risk," *McKinsey Quarterly*, August 1, 2012.

6. D. Lovallo, P. Viguerie, R. Uhlaner, and J. Horn, "Deals Without Delusions," *Harvard Business Review*, December 2007.

7. M. Baghai, S. Coley, D. White, C. Conn, and R. McLean, "Staircases to Growth," *McKinsey Quarterly*, November 1996.

8. N. Taleb, *The Black Swan: The Impact of the Highly Improbable* (New York: Random House, 2007).

9. A. Duke, *Thinking in Bets* (New York: Penguin, 2018).

10. P. Tetlock and D. Gardner, *Superforecasting: The Art and Science of Prediction* (New York: Crown, 2015).

11. CB Insights, "Everything You Need to Know about What Amazon Is Doing in Financial Services," August 2022.

12. A. Jassy, "Amazon 2021 Letter to Shareholders," April 14, 2022, https://www.aboutamazon.com/news/company-news/2021-letter-to-shareholders.

13. A team of five CSIRO astrophysicists and radio engineers led by Dr. John O'Sullivan brought together the combination of techniques that enable high-speed wireless transmission of data and that led to high-speed Wi-Fi as we know it today. For those interested in the invention, US Patent 5,483,069 was filed in 1993 and granted in 1996, and expired in 2013.

14. Personal communication with Catherine Livingstone.

15. E. Dixon, *Sports Pro Insider Blog*, April 20, 2021.

16. J. Scott, *Athletic Business*, June 2020.

17. Personal communication with Richard Atkinson, CFO, AELTC.

18. Ibid.

19. M. Janda, *ABC News*, March 23, 2021.

20. Technically, Kymriah is a genetically modified autologous T-cell immunotherapy, which some observers term a cell therapy, as the gene modification takes place outside the patient's body.

21. D. Thomas, D. Chancellor, A. Micklus, et al., *Clinical Development Success Rates and Contributing Factors 2011–2020* (UK: BIO, Informa, and QLS, 2021).

22. K. Snider, "Four Phases of Clinical Research Studies," UCB, October 1, 2018, https://www.ucb-usa.com/stories-media/UCB-U-S-News/detail/article/ Four-Phases-of-Clinical-Research-Studies.

23. Thomas et al., *Clinical Development Success Rates.*

24. C. H. Wong, K. W. Siah, and A. W. Lo, "Estimation of Clinical Trial Success Rates and Related Parameters," *Biostatistics* 20, no. 2 (2019): 273–286.

25. Thomas et al., *Clinical Development Success Rates.*

26. D. Nguyen, "A Tale of Two Cities: The Battle for Kymriah," LinkedIn, November 26, 2017, https://www.linkedin.com/pulse/tale-two-cities-battle- kymriah-deborah-nguyen/.

27. One might expect that the impressive results of Kymriah in treating the cancer of patients would translate to large revenues for Novartis. However, in the first quarter of 2018, the treatment generated only $12 million, approximately four times below analysts' expectations. Kymriah is initially approved to treat children with acute lymphoblastic leukemia, which affects fewer than 5,000 new patients each year. Kymriah targets just the 30% of these patients who don't respond to regular treatment, such as chemotherapy, immunotherapy, and bone marrow transplants. It is also very expensive, at $475,000 per patient. In the final quarter of 2020, Kymriah sales grew to $141 million, but it still hasn't penetrated Novartis's top-20 drug franchises. J. Carroll, "5 years later, CAR-T pioneer Kymriah offers jaw-dropping evidence of durable remissions—even as it still proves a tough sell," *Endpoints News*, February 18, 2021, https://endpts. com/5-years-later-car-t-pioneer-kymriah-offers-jaw-dropping-evidence-of- durable-remissions-even-as-it-still-proves-a-tough-sell/.

28. H. Jung, A. Engelberg, and A. Kesselheim, "Do large pharma companies provide drug development innovation? Our analysis says no," *STAT*, December 10, 2019, https://www.statnews.com/2019/12/10/large-pharma-companies-provide- little-new-drug-development-innovation/#Table1.

29. Duke, *Thinking in Bets.*

Chapter 6 Show and Tell

1. B. Marshall, "Curiosity Driven Research," Speech, University of Western Australia, 2015.

2. B. Marshall, "Helicobacter Connections," Nobel Lecture, December 8, 2005.

3. A simple breath test, the Urea Breath Test, is now commonly used to detect the presence of *Helicobacter pylori.*

4. Personal communication with Professor Barry Marshall, June 1, 2021.

5. E. Schmidt, "Google CEO Compares Data Across Millennia," *The Atlantic*, July 3, 2010. Much more data is produced in 2022 than 2010.

6. For a wonderful example in Economics, see D. M. Grether and C. R. Plott, "Economic Theory of Choice and the Preference Reversal Phenomenon," *The American Economic Review* 69, no. 4 (1979): 623–638, http://www.jstor.org/stable/1808708.

7. T. Kuhn, *The Structure of Scientific Revolutions* (Chicago: University of Chicago Press, 1962).

8. E. Kopf, (1978). "Florence Nightingale as a Statistician," *Research in Nursing and Health* 1, no. 3 (1978): 93–102.

9. Ibid.

10. H. Martineau, *England and Her Soldiers* (Cambridge, UK: Cambridge University Press, 1859).

11. T. Harford, *The Data Detective* (New York: Riverhead Books, 2021).

12. We first encountered this graphic in Edward Tufte's wonderful book, *The Visual Display of Quantitative Information* (Cheshire, CT: Graphics Press, 1983), the absolute classic text for this space of knockout visuals. We accessed the image on Wikimedia Commons (https://commons.wikimedia.org/wiki/File:Minard.png).

13. Private communication with Rich Gilmore and Dr. Chris Gillies, The Nature Conservancy Australia.

14. J. Gribbin and M. Gribbin, *Richard Feynman: A Life in Science* (New York: Viking, 1997).

15. Ibid.

16. Presidential Commission on the Space Shuttle Challenger Accident (1986). Chapter IV, "The Cause of the Accident," June 1986.

17. Private communication with Don Watters, September 29, 2022.

18. Interview, "Ted Hall Robs a Bank," *Journal of Problem Solving*, 2011.

19. G. Lakoff, *Don't Think of An Elephant, Know Your Values* (White River Junction, VT: Chelsea Green Publishing, 2004).

20. J. Haidt, *The Righteous Mind* (New York: Penguin, 2012).

21. K. Hayhoe, *Saving Us: A Climate Scientist's Case for Hope and healing in a Divided World* (New York: One Signal Publishers, 2021).

22. L. Chen, "Persuasion in Chinese Culture: A Glimpse of the Ancient Practice in Contrast to the West," *Intercultural Communication Studies* XIV: 1 (2005).

23. M. Zakaras, "From Coal to Clean Energy: Welcome to the New Appalachian Economy," *Forbes*, May 26, 2022.

Chapter 7 Epilogue: All Strategies Are Wagers

1. B. Pascal, *Pensées* (New York: Penguin, 1995), 229.

2. Our friend Professor Barry Nalebuff reminded us of a similar wager made by Nobel Prize winner Niels Bohr, but this one with less asymmetric payoffs: "It is said that a visitor once came to Professor Bohr's home and, having noticed a horseshoe hung above the entrance, asked incredulously if the professor believed horseshoes brought good luck. 'No,' Bohr replied, 'but I am told that they bring luck even to those who do not believe in them.'"

3. A. Duke, *Thinking in Bets* (New York: Penguin, 2018).

4. H. Simon, *Models of Man* (New York: Wiley, 1957).

5. Jeff Bezos, "Annual Letter to Shareholders," Amazon, 2015.

6. "The Story of One of the Most Memorable Marketing Blunders Ever: The History of New Coke," Coca-Cola Company, 2022, www.coca-colacompany.com/company/history (accessed July 3, 2022).

7. D. Lovallo, T. Koller, R. Uhlaner, and D. Kahneman, "Your Company Is Too Risk-Averse," *Harvard Business Review*, March–April 2020.

8. N. Taleb, *The Black Swan: The Impact of the Highly Improbable* (New York: Random House, 2007).

9. D. Kahneman and D. Lovallo, "Timid Choices and Bold Forecasts: A Cognitive Perspective on Risk Taking," *Management Science* 39, no.1 (1993): 17–31.

10. J. Kay, and M. King, *Radical Uncertainty* (New York: W.W. Norton, 2020).

11. E. Angner, "Epistemic Humility—Knowing Your Limits in a Pandemic," *Behavioral Scientist*, April 13, 2020.

12. B. Obama, *A Promised Land* (New York: Penguin Books, 2020).

13. H. Courtney, J. Kirkland, and S. P. Viguerie, "Strategy Under Uncertainty," *McKinsey Quarterly*, June 1, 2000.

Acknowledgments

The authors have benefited enormously from interacting with problem-solving colleagues over 30 years in many different walks of life, business, new ventures, nonprofit, and environmental conservation. Creative problem solving works best with critical friends who test your thinking, and we have had many. Our memories are imperfect, so apologies in advance for any accidentally omitted.

First, we must thank Adam de Picot, a budding polymath who started as a researcher but became a real partner in the work over these two years. Thank you, Adam, from the bottom of our hearts.

We overcame COVID-19 travel restrictions by assembling a virtual team of brilliant young research associates at the University of Sydney, including Will Burns, Rosie Adams, Temana Short, Olivia Taylor, and Finn Ball. We are also very grateful to Will Cesta of St. Andrews College at Sydney University, who not only oversaw our research students, but made substantial contributions to our thinking about curiosity.

The book benefited from the critical attention of many readers and advisors, especially Professor Dan Lovallo of the University of Sydney, Professor Barry Nalebuff of Yale, Professor Sally Cripps, formerly of the University of Sydney, Nobel Laureate Barry Marshall, Sir Ronald Cohen, Dr. Peter Farrell, Aidan McCullen, Eric Schmidt, Nicolas Berggruen, Yvon and Malinda Chouinard, Mehrdad Baghai, Chris Bradley, Rik Kirkland, Ted Hall, Kathryn Fagg, Don Watters, Alex Fischer, Professor Robert Wood, Nigel Poole, Catherine Livingstone, Alison Watkins, Siobhan McKenna, Duncan Peppercorn, and Rich Gilmore.

Over time we have learned so much about problem-solving mindsets under uncertainty from former colleagues at McKinsey (David White, John Stuckey, Dominic Barton, and many others), the Moore Foundation and its grantees (Aileen Lee, Ivan Thompson, Michael Webster, Pic Walker, Erin Dovichin, Aaron and Julia Hill, Greg Knox, and Mark Beere), The Nature Conservancy (Jennifer Morris, Marianne Kleiberg, Chuck Cook, Nancy Mackinnon, James Fitzsimons, and Mark Zimring), Patagonia (the Chouinard family, Kris Tompkins, Dan Emmett, Ryan Gellert, Ayana Johnson, Hilary Dessouky, Greg Curtis, Jenna Johnson, Jenna Wells, Matt Dwyer, and many others), Monograph (Fred Cohen, Travis Murdoch, Tim

Funnell, Bonnie van Wilgenburg, and the rest of the team), and in other ventures, including Thomas Layton, Jake Peters, Charlie Lindsay, Michael Bungay Stanier, Andrew Nevin, Sir John Bell, Professor Justin Stebbing, Sir John Hood, Jess Glennie, Paul Shapiro, Lord David Prior, Andrew Kassoy, and Jason Scott.

The team at 5V Capital led by Adrian Mackenzie and Srdjan Dangubic ran a masterclass on imperfectionism during COVID-19 that we learned greatly from. They intuitively adopted the six mindsets, showed they understand Type I and II errors, ran experiments in portfolio companies like Education Perfect, and stepped into risk with small steps followed by bigger ones to create optionality. Zetaris founder Vinay Samuel opened our eyes to the opportunity to stand on the shoulders of others with open source software and collective intelligence. At the Paul Ramsay Foundation colleagues Glyn Davis, Greg Hutchinson, Jeni Whalan, Jenny Tran, Michael Traill, and Professor Kristy Muir stepped into risk in planning big bets in philanthropy, an imperfectionist approach that is rooted in system change understanding.

We learned from northern Australian Indigenous elder Otto Campion about "right way fire" and created a new branch of collective intelligence we term *ancestral wisdom*. And we were able to meet Aiden, a teenager on the autism spectrum who brought the power of a neurodiverse lens to building a digital twin of a kelp forest.

We are grateful to our friends at G01, a compelling online learning platform, who pushed us to think harder about how to teach problem solving, including Andrew Barnes, Cameron Cliff, Phill Deacon, Christopher Joannou, Eliza Allard, and others. We want to thank Tim McLean for his effective marketing of our *Bulletproof Problem Solving* book and for managing all aspects of our digital presence.

We also learned from our audiences and students at the Schmidt Science Fellowship, the Rhodes Scholarship, the Kauffman Venture Fellowship, the Rise Scholarship, World Economic Forum Global Shapers, Roche, Klarna, Genesis SA, Oxford, Harvard, the Australian Graduate School of Management, the Mumbai Business School, the Birla Institute of Technology, and many others. Some of the keenest insights came from those who teach problem solving at other institutions, including Andrew Ogilvie at USC, Hugh Courtney at Northeastern, and Nick Lovegrove at Georgetown University.

We love good graphics, and are so fortunate to have the incredibly talented Nicole Gilroy illustrating this work. James de Vries assisted with layout and design. We had wonderful editorial help from Paula McLean, who constantly reminded us to write clean lines and tell good stories. We are especially grateful to David Schwartz and Timothy Dickson, editors and friends who clarified our thinking and vastly improved our writing.

Finally, a warm thanks to Bill Falloon, Purvi Patel, Pradesh Kumar Chandran, Stacey Rivera, and the team from Wiley, who have been wonderful partners in this problem-solving journey.

This book is dedicated to Paula McLean, and Rob's children, Heather, Ginny, and Tim; and to Camilla Borg, and Charles's children, Hannah, Cameron, and Alexander.

About the Authors

Robert McLean, AM

Rob McLean is a Director Emeritus of McKinsey & Company. He led the Australian and New Zealand McKinsey practice for eight years and served on the firm's global Director's Committee. As Dean of the Australian Graduate School of Management (AGSM), Rob saw the growing need for stronger problem-solving capability for leaders of the future. He is a trustee of The Nature Conservancy in Australia and Asia, and a director of the Paul Ramsay Foundation, Australia's largest philanthropic foundation. He is an advisory board member of 5V Capital and an investor in software and education ventures. Rob is a graduate of the University of New England in Australia and the Columbia University Graduate School of Business. He became a member of the Order of Australia in 2010 for his contributions to business, social welfare, and the environment. In 2019 he co-authored *Bulletproof Problem Solving: The One Skill That Changes Everything* with Charles Conn.

Charles Conn

Charles Conn is a cross-sector leader, conservationist, and entrepreneur. He is co-founding partner of Monograph Capital, a life sciences venture investment firm in London and San Francisco. He was CEO of Oxford Sciences Innovation, a £600 million venture firm formed in partnership with Oxford University. Charles was a technology entrepreneur, and as founding CEO of Ticketmaster-Citysearch led the company through its IPO and acquisitions of Match.com and other companies. He is also a nonprofit education and conservation leader, including as CEO of the Rhodes Trust, which provides the Rhodes Scholarships in Oxford. Prior to his Oxford roles, Charles was senior advisor to the Gordon & Betty Moore Foundation, where he led conservation projects including the wild salmon ecosystems initiative and the Palmyra atoll research station. He sits or has sat on many company and nonprofit boards, including Patagonia, where he is chair, the Mandela Rhodes Foundation in South Africa, and The Nature Conservancy European Council. He began his career at McKinsey & Company, where he was a partner. He is a graduate of Harvard Business School, Boston University, and Oxford University, where he was a Rhodes Scholar.

Index

Page numbers followed by *e* refer to exhibits.